Jim Bowen and Bobby Bowden

To Sylvia
Best Wishes.
Jim Bow

"In June of 1955 I accepted my first head coaching job at South Georgia College…So at the age of 25, we, my wife, Ann (22), plus our children Robyn, Steve, and Tommy (ages 5 to 1 year), loaded up our '51 Chevy coup and headed for Douglas, Georgia, the home of South Georgia College. I coached there for 4 years, '55, '56, '57, and '58. I met the greatest bunch of players in those years I have ever been around. In 2008 we celebrated our 52-year reunion together. We do it every year. Jimmy Bowen has put together this book, so I'll let him tell you 'the rest of the story.'"

—Bobby Bowden, Head Football Coach, Florida State University

Memories of a Legend and His Boys from South Georgia College

B O B B Y
BOWDEN

Memories of a Legend and His Boys from South Georgia College

JIM BOWEN

Cold Tree Press
Nashville, Tennessee

Cold Tree Press is an independent, traditional, trade paperback press committed to introducing fresh, exciting voices to the reading public. It is our mission to take a chance on deserving authors and achieve the highest quality when bringing their words to the marketplace. We believe in the power of words and ideas and strive to introduce readers to new, creative writers.

A TRADITIONAL
TRADE PAPERBACK PRESS

Published by Cold Tree Press, Nashville, Tennessee

Copyright © 2008 Jim Bowen

Cover Design © 2008 Cold Tree Press
Interior Design by Bobby Dawson
Coach Bobby Bowden photograph courtesy of FSU Sports Information
Interior Photographs courtesy of Jim Bowen

Manufactured in the United States of America

10 9   8   7   6   5   4   3   2   1

Library of Congress Number: 2008909806

ISBN-13: 978-1-58385-282-8
ISBN-10: 1-58385-282-4

This book is dedicated to the
"Boys from South Georgia College"
who played football for
the legendary Coach Bobby Bowden
and are now spending eternity with our Heavenly Father.

TABLE OF CONTENTS

FOREWORD
by Vince Gibson

I HAVE KNOWN COACH BOWDEN FOR MOST OF MY LIFE. We were both born and raised in Birmingham, Alabama, and attended high school and college together. My earliest memory of him took place when I was about twelve years old and he was about fifteen. As youngsters we used to play pickup football on the football field at Howard College, and on this particular day there was an older boy playing with us that was bullying me and some of the other younger kids. This upset Bobby, who was a good boxer, and he gave the bully a beating that he probably never forgot. Bobby became a hero to me and all the other kids in the neighborhood that day, and he has been my idol ever since.

Later, I went to Woodlawn High School with him and his future wife, Ann Estock, and we became close friends. As far back as I can remember, Ann has always been instrumental in his life and supported him in everything that he has done. As we all know, behind every successful man is a great woman, and Bobby Bowden is no exception. In high school, Ann was a cheerleader and Bobby was an outstanding running back on the football team.

After high school, Bobby and I played football together at Howard College, and Bobby made Little All-American as a quarterback his senior year. During those days he was so quick and agile that it was fun just watching him scramble all over the field while the bigger linemen tried to catch him. By then he was already a role model for a lot of young men who looked up to him, not only because he was a great football player, but because he was always a reliable friend and influential leader in the school. He was also a very religious person, and his actions clearly demonstrated his strong Christian beliefs as well as his concerns for his fellow students.

When Bobby graduated from Howard, I was only a sophomore. I transferred to Florida State University to finish my degree and graduated in the spring of 1955. After I graduated, I immediately accepted an assistant coaching job at a high school in St. Augustine, Florida, got married, and moved to St. Augustine where I anticipated that I would be coaching when school started in the fall. During the summer, however, before that happened, Bobby drove to St. Augustine and talked me into being his assistant at South Georgia College.

Bobby has always been a great recruiter, and after he talked me into moving to South Georgia to be his assistant, I knew that recruiting would always be his forte. The school in St. Augustine had already promised me a salary of $4,500 a year—and if I recall correctly, that was about what Bobby was making at South Georgia. When he convinced me to become his assistant at South Georgia, I took a $900 per year pay cut.

Later, I found out that when Bobby left St. Augustine and drove back to South Georgia, he had to drive about a hundred miles out of his way because he didn't even have fifty cents in his pockets to pay the toll at a bridge in Jacksonville. Apparently he didn't want me to know just how difficult it was to live on the salary that I would be making at South Georgia, or he was too proud to borrow the money from me. When I learned this, I obviously felt a lot more secure about my financial future.

As it turned out, my move to South Georgia was probably the best move that I ever made in my coaching career. Many of the players there were Korean War veterans and were as old as or older than Bobby and I, and we had a special relationship with them. Even today many of those players are still an important part of Bobby's and my life.

One of my favorite stories about South Georgia occurred

when Bobby came to me in a panic one day and told me that he had given out more scholarships than were allotted in our budget. We talked about it for awhile, but Bobby never said what he was going to do to correct the situation. Shortly after that, however, we lost our first game, so Bobby called a squad meeting and the first thing he asked our players was how many of them had broken training over the weekend. There was suddenly complete silence in the room, and everyone started looking around at each other. Finally, after what seemed like several minutes, one by one, a few players started raising their hands. To the best of my memory, Billy "Stumpy" Franklin was the first one. Then about half the team put their hands up. Once the hands stopped rising, Bobby said to them, "All you guys are off scholarship."

That incident cost Bobby and me big-time because none of our players would ever raise their hands for anything else for the rest of that year. As it turned out though, no one lost his scholarship and we won the Georgia junior college championship.

While Bobby and I were at South Georgia, he was the head football and baseball coach, and I was the head basketball and track coach and his assistant during football season. I also taught the girls' PE class twice a week, and Bobby taught the boys'. To this day, I believe that Bobby assigned me the girls' class because Ann wouldn't let him teach the girls.

Bobby and I have both had long and successful careers in the coaching profession and have coached at several colleges and universities over the years. And even though South Georgia was a junior college and my first coaching job, I can say without any reservations that I loved and enjoyed my years there the most. I also know that Bobby feels the same way.

Everyone knows that Bobby Bowden has been and is still an incredible football coach, but in my opinion, he is an even greater person. Success has never changed him, and he has never forgotten the people he grew up with in high school, college, and, in particular, South Georgia College. He has always been as caring and respectful of his fellow man as he is religious, and that has surely been the hallmark of this great man. He was my idol when we were growing up and he still is today.

Vince Gibson started his coaching career with Bobby Bowden at South Georgia Junior College. Over the years, he has been the head football coach at Kansas State University, University of Louisville, and Tulane University. Gibson retired from coaching in 1982 and has since been enshrined in the Alabama Sports Hall of Fame and the Kansas State University Athletics Hall of Fame.

INTRODUCTION

RARELY ARE INDIVIDUALS' LIVES so extraordinary or their accomplishments so remarkable that they are recognized as legends after death. Even fewer are viewed as legends while they are still alive. This is the story of one such individual, a living legend, whose legacy has been developing for more than five decades and continues to grow even today. It's the story about a remarkable man whose career and work for a period of more than fifty years have affected the lives of thousands of young men in a very positive way. It's the story of an individual who reconciled his boyhood dreams with God's purpose for his life by choosing to coach football and build character and integrity in his players. It's also a story about a group of young men, many just returning from military service and the Korean War, and their experiences playing for a young coach when he was just beginning his journey into greatness. More than anything else, it's a story about relationships among men that have lasted and grown for more than one half century. Finally, it's a collection of memories of the legendary football coach, Bobby Bowden, and his "Boys from South Georgia College."

01
THE LEGEND:
COACH BOBBY BOWDEN

An intelligent, charismatic, Christian gentleman named Robert Cleckler Bowden, affectionately called Coach Bobby Bowden by thousands of football fans throughout America, has been unwittingly building his legacy for more than fifty years. In the beginning, for almost two decades, he toiled at small colleges or in assistant coaching positions, fine-tuning his skills while patiently following what he believed was God's plan for his life. The metamorphosis from obscure small-college football coach to big-time prominence was a slow, laborious process that finally peaked when he accepted the head coach position at Florida State University in 1976.

Since that day, with the passing of each year, he has accelerated his ascent to the top of the tallest mountain in the arena of big-time college football. In January 2006 he completed his thirtieth year as the head coach of the FSU Seminoles. Thirty years at the same university is rarely achieved in today's extremely competitive world of college football. This particular triumph, however, is only one of this remarkable man's outstanding achievements.

When he first took the reins at FSU in 1976, he inherited a frequently maligned program that was far different from the dynasty he now commands. In fact, it was so near disaster that many of its fans and supporters believed it was on a collision course with extinction. The Seminoles' football team had struggled over the previous four years to win a mere four games. As a result of their unimpressive record during that period and their frequent uninspiring play, most of their home games were played in a nearly empty stadium, which created a huge financial burden on the university's athletic program. Fans and alumni alike were rapidly turning their backs on a football program that had been a disappointment and embarrassment to the entire university for several years. There were even rumors that some university officials were seriously questioning whether football at Florida State should continue, and many in its hierarchy were leaning toward its elimination.

Even though Bowden was acutely aware of this seemingly hopeless situation, he accepted the head coach position when it was offered to him, which surprised fans and sports writers. They asked themselves why anyone would want to take over a football program that was obviously on the slippery slope to being obliterated. It was unimaginable to any of them that he accepted it for any of the usual reasons—more money or more opportunity. To their thinking, it had to be a reason that only he understood.

It was, in fact, a decision he made the same way he made most of his major decisions since becoming an adult. He prayed about it, discussed it with his family, and then took the job because he felt God was leading him to Florida State.

Once he accepted the FSU position, the few fans who had hung with the Seminoles through their toughest times began to get excited. They, however, were in the minority. To the vast majority of past FSU supporters, it already seemed too late; no one could change the direction of their failing program. Many skeptics even went so far as to state that Bowden had probably jeopardized his own future by accepting the FSU job and expecting to resurrect a program that was already predestined to fail.

Even the most optimistic couldn't believe that anyone could turn the Seminoles' program around and make it a winner anytime in the foreseeable future.

Amid these negative attitudes, Bowden pushed forward, accepting another challenge prayerfully, optimistically, and determinedly. With his innately positive attitude and strong belief that he was following a plan ordained by God, he developed a blueprint to succeed—The Bowden Way.

Once he and his staff began to implement the strategy he had outlined, amazing things happened. Beginning with their first season, which was just a few months after he walked onto the playing field at Doak S. Campbell Stadium, the Seminoles started winning. They won more games that year than they had won the previous four years together. It was the first winning season for the Seminoles in almost a decade. The second year was even more impressive, and almost unbelievable, because they won 10 games and were invited to play in a post-season bowl game. The third year mirrored the second and was equally successful. The fourth year was the most amazing year of all and clearly exceeded every fan and supporter's wildest dreams.

In just four short years, the FSU football team, once considered one of the worst Division 1-A teams in the nation, finished the season within one game of a national championship: a four-year run no one—not one player, coach, university official, alumnus, fan, or sports writer —would have ever believed possible when Bowden took the helm.

The team's revival brought the skeptics who had walked away from Seminoles' football stampeding back. More than that, the unbelievable turnaround fulfilled the childhood dreams of a man whose humble beginnings at a small college in southern Georgia were just two decades behind him.

But to his many friends and colleagues, Bowden's success was just another example of how this uniquely inspiring man, who lives every day of his life seeking God's will, paved the way to his success.

The job at Florida State was Bowden's fourth head coach position since he began his head coaching career at South Georgia Junior College in 1955. At South Georgia, in a period of four years, his teams won two state junior college conference championships, tied for a third, and were runners-up for another. His second job was at his alma mater, Howard College, in Birmingham, Alabama, which was the same job he had applied for but was denied four years earlier because the president at Howard thought Bowden was too young and lacked the necessary experience to be a head coach.

This time, however, he didn't have to apply; he was sought out and offered the job by Howard's new president, partially because of his success at South Georgia. After he accepted the position at Howard College, he coached there for four years, from 1959 through 1962, and his teams won thirty-one games and lost only six. In a very short period, he managed to move Howard's football program from the depths of obscurity into the limelight of small-college football.

His years at Howard were bittersweet. Bitter because even after completing four very successful seasons, he realized Howard would never play Division 1 football, and coaching a Division 1 team was one of his dreams. The sweet part was that his success at Howard gave him the exposure he needed to get Coach Bill Peterson's attention at Florida State University and eventually get an invitation, in 1963, to join his staff.

Once he joined Peterson's staff, he quickly developed a reputation as an offensive wizard. As his reputation continued to grow, he began receiving other, more lucrative offers. Two years later, in 1966, Coach Jim Carlen, the head coach at West Virginia University, convinced him to leave Florida State and move to WVU to be his offensive coordinator. After Bowden took over the offensive program, the Mountaineers won the majority of their games. Four years later, in 1970, Carlen resigned and Bowden was selected as his replacement. He remained at WVU as head coach for another six years.

In those six years, the Mountaineers won 42 games and lost 26 in a very competitive conference. They were also invited to play in several post-season bowl games. Those stats caught the eye of several universities whose football programs were struggling for recognition. One of those universities was Florida State, whose program had been in a downward spiral since Bowden left ten years before.

In 1976, Bowden decided to accept the biggest challenge of his coaching career and return to FSU. Since that date, he has steadily built his legacy and accomplished what many Florida State supporters are still struggling to comprehend.

One of Bowden's greatest accomplishments was Florida State's ranking by the Associated Press as one of the top five football teams in the nation for fourteen consecutive seasons. This was such an unprecedented accomplishment that it has never been equaled by any other Division 1-A coach or football team.

Bowden's FSU teams have also won two national championships: one in 1993 and another in 1999. In addition, they finished second in the nation in 1987 and 1992. In both of those years, they played in a nationally televised playoff game for the championship. They finished third in the nation in 1988, 1989, 1997, and 1998; fourth in 1990, 1991, 1994, 1995, and 1996; and fifth in 2002. No team in college football history can match that winning consistency.

In 1993, Florida State became a member of the Atlantic Coast Conference, one of the strongest football conferences in the country at the time. Since joining that conference, their football teams have won ten ACC Championships, and Bowden has been named the conference's coach of the year twice: first in 1993 and then again in 1997.

In 2002, when Florida State defeated the Virginia Tech Hokies in the Gator Bowl in their last game of the season, Bowden earned his 332nd coaching victory—which didn't include his 22 wins at South Georgia—and tied him with one of his lifelong coaching idols, Coach Paul "Bear" Bryant. Once he reached this milestone, there was only one major college football coach remaining with more recorded victories than Bowden: Coach Joe Paterno, the current and still active head coach at Penn State University. Paterno finished the 2002 season with 336 career wins.

On October 25, 2003, as Coach Bowden continued his quest to become the winningest coach in the history of Division 1-A football, he leapfrogged Paterno and reached what many considered the apex of his coaching career. On that memorable Saturday afternoon, the FSU Seminoles defeated the Wake Forest Deacons 48-24 in Tallahassee, Florida.

That win gave Bowden 339 victories and broke a one-week deadlock with Paterno. Since then, Bowden has stood alone—ahead of a list of great legendary coaches like Paul "Bear" Bryant, Glenn "Pop" Warner, Amos Alonzo Stagg, and, of course, Joe Paterno.

Since 2003 the Seminoles have won 41 more games (10 in 2003, 9 in 2004, 8 in 2005, 7 in 2006, and 7 in 2007), giving Bowden a grand total of 373 wins over a forty-three year period. With these victories, he is still the winningest coach in Division 1-A.

In recognition of his talent, he was awarded the Southern Independent Coach of the Year Award in 1977, the National Coach of the Year Award by ABC Sports in 1979, the Bobby Dodd Coach of the Year Award in 1980, and the Region II Coach of the Year Award in 1987. In 1983 he was inducted into the Florida Sports Hall of Fame, and in 1987 he was also inducted into the Alabama Sports Hall of Fame.

Two of his most recent accolades came in 2004 when Florida State University named the playing field at Doak S. Campbell Stadium the "Bobby Bowden Field" and erected a large bronze statue of him at one of the stadium's entrances. The last and one of the most prestigious awards came on December 5, 2006, when he was inducted into the College Football Hall of Fame.

Although Bowden has received an untold number of awards and accolades during the past fifty-plus years, he has never deviated from his initial convictions: to win with integrity, to always play by the rules of a higher power, and to live by and set the highest moral standards in everything he does. With these convictions as his guide, he has consistently and persistently inspired thousands of young men to always reach for their greatest goals by having faith in God and believing in themselves.

In chapter thirty-two of the book *More Than Just a Game,* written by Bill Smith and published in 1994, Bowden was asked, "What's it like to be a legend?" His response was typical: "Legend? I'm no more a dad-gum legend than the man in the moon." But, according to The American Heritage Dictionary, New College Edition, a legend is "a person who has achieved legendary fame," and without question, Florida State's football coach Bobby Bowden has achieved legendary fame. It would be unimaginable, if not impossible to find anyone in this country who knows anything about college football who doesn't recognize the name Bobby Bowden, or who would argue that he is not famous. Consequently, the term "legend" and the name "Bobby Bowden" are synonymous in the annals of college football history.

A remarkable accomplishment by an amazing man who started his ascension to the top of his profession five decades earlier from the sandy flatlands of southern Georgia and a small college known as South Georgia Junior College.

02

SOUTH GEORGIA COLLEGE
AND THE TIGERS' EARLY HISTORY

South Georgia College, where Bobby Bowden started his head coaching career in 1955, is the oldest state-supported two-year college in the state of Georgia. It is located in the small town of Douglas, approximately seventy miles north of the Florida state line and only about 250 feet above sea level, making it very flat and sandy.

Throughout the early part of the twentieth century, the majority of the residents of the Douglas area made their living either by farming or supporting farming.

In the earliest part of that century, the state of Georgia didn't have a state-supported public high school system, so most Georgia teenagers didn't go to school past the seventh or eighth grade. In 1906, in an effort to change this shortcoming and offer better educational opportunities, the Georgia General Assembly passed legislation that created a school in each of the twelve congressional districts. These new schools would be known as District Agricultural and Mechanical Schools and were to be strategically situated throughout the state. In keeping with the times, the curriculum was required to be primarily related to agriculture and mechanical subjects.

While this legislation was being finalized and approved, the citizens of Douglas realized that a district school was badly needed in their community, so they came together and made an offer to the state they felt would guarantee that their town, which was made up of fewer than one thousand citizens, would be one of the twelve sites selected for one of the new schools. In their offer, one of Douglas' most prominent citizens, Mr. Benajah Peterson, agreed to donate three hundred acres of land to be used for the school's campus.

Douglas citizens also agreed to construct three buildings to house the school's activities. It was estimated that these three buildings would cost about $52,000. They also agreed to provide the school with water and electricity for ten years. Today, one of the three original buildings still bears Peterson's name: Peterson Hall.

During the latter part of 1906, the state made its final selections, and the residents of Douglas were officially notified that their town would be the site for the Eleventh District A&M School. The following year, during construction, a young man named Joseph M. Thrash, a recent graduate of the Georgia Institute of Technology in Atlanta, was contracted by the state to oversee the building process and ultimately the completion of the school.

While overseeing construction, Thrash began to see real potential in the school. He became a faculty member once the school was completed, which turned out to be one of the most significant events in the history of the district school and South Georgia College.

The district school concept had been in operation for approximately twenty years when the Georgia General Assembly decided it was time for the state to start building and funding a more uniform and comprehensive system of public high schools. To accomplish their mandate, the state immediately started building new schools and consolidating some of the district schools. Thrash was quick to realize that this spelled the end for the Eleventh District A&M School, so he started looking for another way to utilize the school's campus. Being a visionary, he decided the area's most pressing need was an educational institution that went beyond the high school level. In his opinion, converting the current A&M school into a junior college was the most logical step.

To his surprise, he soon discovered that his enthusiasm was not shared by all community leaders, most notably some influential politicians whose support he thought he needed to make his initiative become a reality. But Thrash fought back and successfully ran for the state legislature.

After being sworn into the Georgia General Assembly in 1926, one of his first official acts was to introduce a bill known as the "Thrash Bill." The bill incorporated his ideas for turning the Eleventh District A&M School into a state-supported junior college. With the support of his colleagues, the Thrash Bill was passed, and the conversion began.

The transitional period lasted approximately five years, from 1927 to 1932. During this period, the school functioned simultaneously as a high school and a junior college. The high school continued to be known as the Eleventh District A&M School and the college became known as South Georgia State Junior College. Thrash, who was already serving as the high school principal, was given the additional duties of acting college president. For the next four years, he performed the duties of high school principal, acting college president, and district representative in the state legislature.

Once the transition was completed, the school's name was shortened to South Georgia College and it officially became an independent junior college, completely separate from the original A&M school, and Thrash was appointed its first president.

Many of South Georgia's original supporters and most of its first faculty members believe that Thrash's greatest contribution to South Georgia was during this period. His unrelenting determination to make the college a success against a barrage of seemingly insurmountable obstacles was, in their opinion, an even greater accomplishment than his incredible initiative to create the college.

Faculty members from those days believed that South Georgia was Thrash's greatest love and that he held a special weakness for its athletic teams—especially football. They remember that he always encouraged the school's staff and students to support their athletic programs. And because of his encouragement, South Georgia's football, basketball, and baseball teams were always very competitive.

In its infancy, the school's leadership and student body selected "Tigers" for their teams' mascot and purple and gold for their school colors.

In 1933, President Thrash hired M.E. "Mike" Herndon as South Georgia's first full-time head coach and athletic director. Herndon came to South Georgia from Valdosta High School, where he had built one of the strongest high school football programs in the state. Although Herndon was hired primarily to coach football, he quickly learned, like so many other coaches who followed him, that he had to coach basketball and baseball too. Under his leadership, South Georgia consistently won the majority of their athletic contests— their football games especially.

George A. Gaines, a member of South Georgia's 1938 and 1939 class, and Nathan H. Acker, a member of its 1940 and 1941 class, both played football for Herndon and fondly remember him as an outstanding coach, a gentleman, and a great leader for the young men who played for him. A 1940-41 South Georgia College bulletin reflected that, "About ninety percent of the graduating letter-men trained by Coach Herndon made four-year college teams after leaving SGC."

Herndon coached football at South Georgia longer than any other coach in its history, from 1933 until Japan attacked Pearl Harbor on December 7, 1941. Football was suspended at South Georgia, and many other colleges and universities across the country, when the United States joined the war against Japan and Germany. Many male students at South Georgia, including just about the entire football team, dropped out of school and enlisted in the armed forces to support the war effort. When this happened, Herndon resigned and returned to coaching football at the high school level.

In 1946, after the war was over and the nation started trying to return to some form of normalcy, South Georgia resumed its football program. John McMillan was selected as its new coach and athletic director. He and about fifty young men began the task of rebuilding the Tigers for the 1946 season. According to a local newspaper, the majority of the team members were ex-servicemen who had recently been released from military service. After that first demanding season, McMillan resigned.

In 1947, McMillan was replaced by Head Coach Wyatt Posey and South Georgia's first full-time assistant coach, Mel Bray. Under the direction of these two new coaches, the Tigers quickly returned to a position of prominence in junior college football, finishing the season with a 7-1-1 record and winning the Eastern Georgia Championship.

Although 1947 was a banner year for the Tigers' football team, it was a sad year for many of its supporters because they lost their most avid fan when President Thrash died.

After Thrash's death, Dr. William S. Smith was selected as South Georgia's new president. Smith's love of sports was not as strong as Thrash's, but he continued to support the school's athletic programs, and most teams continued to thrive and excel. With this continued support, Posey coached four more successful years at South Georgia before resigning after the 1950 season to accept a similar position at Texas A&M in College Station, Texas.

After Posey resigned, Johnny Griffith, South Georgia's first junior college All-American and Posey's assistant in 1950, succeeded Coach Posey and became the Tigers' head coach in 1951. During Griffith's tenure, the Tigers' football teams continued to dominate junior college teams throughout the southeastern United States. That success made it possible for Griffin to resign after the 1953 season to accept a coaching position at a larger four-year college in South Carolina.

When Griffith resigned, Joe Davis, a University of Florida graduate who had recently returned from military service, took the reins at South Georgia for the 1954 season. Sam Mrvos, a recent graduate and former footballer at the University of Georgia, was hired as his assistant. Faced with a difficult schedule that included several four-year colleges, Davis and Mrvos initiated a tough, hard-nosed approach to coaching in order to maintain the winning tradition that

Posey and Griffin had established. The approach, while typical of the era, turned out to be anything but successful for the South Georgia Tigers that year. The grueling physical and mental punishment the coaches imposed did not sit well with members of the team—many of whom were just back from the Korean War—so they quit the team halfway through the season, leaving Davis and Mrvos with so few players that it became almost impossible for them to field a team for South Georgia's last few games.

The school's disappointment was reflected in the student annual, which referred to the 1954 football team's accomplishments by reporting, "The scores for our season were so amazing that we feel it's tactful not to record them for posterity!" At the end of the 1954-1955 school year, Davis resigned.

Shortly after Davis submitted his resignation, President Smith announced that Bobby Bowden had been hired as South Georgia's new head coach and athletic director. With this announcement, South Georgia was destined to return to its dominance in junior college football.

03

THE LEGACY BEGINS:
BOWDEN NAMED HEAD COACH AT SGC

*I*n July 1955 a *local paper*, *The Douglas Enterprise*, reported that Bobby Bowden, a former Little All-American quarterback at Howard College in Birmingham, Alabama, had recently been named by President William Smith as head coach of all sports at South Georgia College. The article was very brief and commanded little attention; however, in its brevity, it did report that Bowden was twenty-five years of age, married, and the father of three children. It also stated that he had been an assistant coach at Howard College prior to accepting the job at South Georgia.

No one reading this small, unpretentious mid-page article could have known, or would have ever imagined, that it was actually announcing the beginning of the greatest legacy in the history of college football: the legacy of Coach Bobby Bowden, the most admired and respected college football coach in America with the most recorded victories in Division I-A. If those who read that unassuming article were to look back at the events that have occurred in Bowden's life since its publication, they'd find it hard not to believe that he was predestined to be at South Georgia College at that particular time in his life.

In fact, it seems that divine intervention not only played a role in his being at South Georgia at that particular time, but also in his selection of coaching as a career and his successes in the grand arena of college football.

Bowden was born on November 8, 1929. His father and mother,

who lived by very strong Christian values, taught him from a young age that God had a plan and purpose for his life, and he should always seek His will.

Bowden still believes this today, and he feels that his belief has been reinforced many times during his lifetime. In a career that has spanned more than fifty years, he has never successfully applied for or sought a head coach position at any college or university. All the positions he has ever held, including his first at South Georgia College and his current position at Florida State University, were offered to him without his seeking them. When he was young and just starting out, he applied for a few head coach positions, but he was never selected to fill any of them. He has said that when he applied for those positions, it was usually because he had decided to follow his own inclinations without first considering God's will.

From his very early boyhood, as far back as he can remember, he was exposed to the game of football in a very positive way. It was a game that he and his father spent many hours watching and playing together. For that reason as much as any other, he always wanted to play or be associated with the game. He was also fortunate enough in his young life to live very close if not immediately adjacent to a high school or college football field. It was Woodlawn High School in Birmingham, Alabama, where he got his first real taste of the game. The second was Howard College, where he made Little All-American as a player and later became one of its most successful head coaches.

Bowden had unlimited opportunities to watch the teams of these two schools practice and play while dreaming about his own future. During every football season, from as early as he can recall, he filled just about all of his free time playing, watching, or thinking about football. When he listened to football games on the radio, he dreamed that one day he might be a part of the sport.

All of this had a big influence on where and what he is today. To many, including Bowden himself, his current position was all part of God's plan—Bowden has always tried to use his dreams to serve Him.

Bowden's early boyhood dreams never wavered until one fateful day in 1943, when he got sick and his doctor discovered that he was suffering from rheumatic fever. Rheumatic fever can be crippling; it can affect the heart, joints, nervous system, and skin, and, especially in 1943, it could also kill. When Bowden was diagnosed with rheumatic fever, medical science had not yet discovered a cure for it. Most physicians treated it by requiring their patients to stay in bed and rest, hoping their immune systems would somehow conquer the illness and they would get well. Bowden's family physician was no exception.

When his doctor first diagnosed the illness, he detected a heart murmur, and Bowden was immediately ordered to go to bed and stay there twenty-four hours a day until his doctor decided he was well enough to get up. His physician ordered that everything he did be done lying flat on his back in bed. He wasn't permitted to get out of bed, or even sit up, for any reason—not even to go to the bathroom.

His physician was extremely concerned that the fever had already affected his heart and that any exertion would kill him or, at the very least, seriously disable him for life. Bowden stayed in bed for almost six months, which, to a thirteen-year-old boy, seemed like eternity.

While he was sick and confined to his bed, many people, including the congregation of the Ruhama Baptist Church where Bowden and his family attended church, were praying for him. The church's pastor came to see him and pray for his recovery almost every day. His illness was considered so serious at the time that his physician told him and his parents that even if he recovered, he would never be able to play any sports again.

This was certainly the lowest point of Bowden's young life. Just as he was about to enter high school and be able to go out for the football team, his life was turned upside down, crushing his dreams.

One evening, while Bowden was lying in bed and his mother was sitting in the bedroom with him, she asked him if he truly believed that God answered prayers. When Bowden told her he did, she suggested he pray for a miracle and ask God to help him get well.

Bowden, of course, had already been praying, but he remembers that this particular time he *really* prayed that God would heal him and make it possible for him to play football. He was a young man praying his heart out, and he promised God that if he ever got well, he would use his life to serve Him. It was the kind of sincere prayer that Christians believe God answers, even though they know He answers on His schedule, not theirs, and according to His will. Bowden didn't get well immediately, but he continued to pray that God would someday help him get healthy again.

Eventually, he began to feel better, and his physician allowed him to sit up in bed and take short walks inside his home. After several more weeks of confinement, he was well enough to return to school, but he was still restricted by his physician from participating in any physical exercise—the one thing he wanted most.

After Bowden returned to school, he had to make up the eighth grade before he could enter Woodlawn High School, which allowed him time to get healthier and stronger. He hoped that by the time he entered high school his physician would change his mind about sports. When he finally completed the eighth grade, however, even though several months had gone by, his physician was still adamant that he should not participate in any athletic activities.

Bowden had a hard time giving up his dream of playing football though, so he continued to pray, even though he was discouraged and sometimes felt his prayers were in vain, or that maybe God had a different plan for him.

Over the next couple of years, Bowden's physician refused to change his prognosis and continued to insist that he should not get involved in any strenuous activities, particularly sports. In his opinion, the activity would be too much for Bowden's heart and would probably kill him.

This obviously scared Bowden and his parents; therefore, during his first two years in high school, he reluctantly accepted what he thought was his fate and joined the school band—thinking that by joining the band, he would at least be supporting the football team, and that by supporting the team, he would in some way lose his nagging desire to be an active player. But, band didn't give him the relief or comfort he had hoped for. Instead, just the opposite occurred. Every time he went onto the field, his dreams were rekindled, and he wanted more than ever to be a part of the football team.

Eventually, during the latter part of the tenth grade, Bowden talked his parents into taking him to a heart specialist for a second opinion. He wasn't optimistic that the outcome would be any different, but something kept telling him that he needed another medical opinion.

After a thorough examination, the specialist told Bowden and his parents that he couldn't find anything but a slight heart murmur that, in his opinion, shouldn't keep Bowden from playing football or doing anything else he wanted to do. This simple but dramatic report gave Bowden such a tremendous sense of relief that he broke down and cried before he left the doctor's office. He and his parents couldn't help but believe that God had answered their prayers.

Going into his junior year in high school, Bowden wasted no time in going out for Woodlawn's football team. He felt that his dreams were finally becoming a reality. And even though he knew he only had two years of high school eligibility remaining, and that two years wasn't much time to make a real impact—especially since he was only 5'6" tall and didn't weigh any more than 130 pounds—he was still happy, and he wasn't about to be deterred or discouraged.

If anything, his size made him more determined to work hard and make the most of his time. His coach, Kenny Morgan, one of the most successful high school coaches in the state of Alabama at the time, must have recognized his enthusiasm as well as his willingness to work hard, because he made Bowden a tailback on a team running a single-wing formation.

In the 1940s, a tailback in a single-wing formation was similar to a quarterback in most of today's offensive formations. He touched the football on almost every offensive play. This was just what Bowden wanted, and his determination and work ethic improved with every practice.

He was living his dream, and things were going pretty well for him until one afternoon at practice about two weeks before their first game. Running a pass route, he slipped and fell, breaking his right thumb. He had to wear a hard, heavy cast on his strongest hand, and it was obvious to him and his coach that he wasn't going to be the most sure-handed player on the field.

Things had suddenly turned from difficult to impossible for Bowden, and it was beginning to look like that old black cloud that had been hanging around for the past few years was back with a vengeance. He would have to miss most of his junior year football season because of his injury.

Bowden was beginning to believe that his dreams of playing football just weren't meant to be. He knew he'd have a hard time making the team when he returned his senior year with no real experience. And even if he did make the team, he probably wouldn't play very much. What he didn't know, but has since learned, is that anything is possible when God has a plan.

SHORTLY AFTER HE GOT HURT and Coach Morgan decided that his injury was going to land him on the bench for most of the season, the coach called Bowden into his office and suggested that he drop out of school until the next semester. Morgan's rationale was that if Bowden dropped out, his injury would have plenty of time to heal, and he would still have two years of eligibility left when he returned. Morgan also explained that when he returned, he would be a year older and would probably have grown some. He also suggested that if Bowden had two years of eligibility remaining when he returned and he continued working hard, he might even get a college scholarship to play football when he graduated.

Bowden seemed excited about the idea, so Morgan approached

Bowden's parents. At first they were reluctant to go along with Morgan's idea. But after prayerfully considering it and seeing how encouraged their son was by the plan, they agreed to let him drop out for one semester.

Later that year when Bowden returned to school and went out for spring football practice, he wasn't much taller, but his weight was up to 150 pounds. The extra weight helped, and he had a successful season his junior year. By his senior year, he was almost 5'8" tall, and his weight was close to 160 pounds. As a result of his extra year of eligibility, Bowden made Birmingham's all-city all-star team his senior year and was offered a scholarship to play football at the University of Alabama.

Before Bowden graduated from high school, he planned to accept Alabama's invitation, but by then another strong force was at work in his life. That force was Ann Estock, his sweetheart, who was still in high school. The thought of being separated from Ann made him change his mind, and instead of going to Alabama, he enrolled at Howard College and went out for their football team. He understood that he was giving up something he had worked for and dreamed about most of his life, but he also knew that he had found the girl he wanted to spend the rest of his life with, and he didn't want to be separated from her or risk losing her by going away to the University of Alabama.

It wasn't long after Bowden enrolled at Howard College that he and Ann eloped to a small town across the Georgia state line and got married. They have now been married for more than fifty-seven years and have six children and twenty-one grandchildren.

Bowden's four years at Howard were busy for him and Ann. In addition to going to school and playing football, he worked part-time to support his growing family, while Ann completed high school and took care of their flock of new babies. Bowden graduated from Howard College and received his bachelor's degree in January 1953. Before he graduated, he and Ann had two small children, Robyn and

Steve, with a third on the way, and Bowden knew he needed to get a full-time job as soon as possible.

While he was trying to decide what to do about his future, he talked to Coach Earl Gartman, Howard's head football coach, about coaching as a full-time occupation. While they were talking, Gartman told Bowden he would hire him as an assistant if he got his master's degree. Bowden immediately got excited because he had already decided he wanted to coach football—at a college if possible.

With Gartman's promise of a job, Bowden enrolled at Peabody College in Nashville, Tennessee, and for the next seven months, he commuted every week to Nashville until he obtained a master's degree in physical education. While he was in school, he and Ann and their children lived with Bowden's parents. After he got his master's degree in the fall of 1953, Gartman, being true to his word, hired him as a member of his staff at Howard College, and Bowden was finally employed full-time in the occupation he had dreamed of for so long.

Howard College was a small Baptist college, and its budget for their football program only allowed for three staff members. Since Bowden was only twenty-three years old and didn't have any coaching experience, he made only $3,600 a year in his assistant coaching position, but he was happy and eager to learn from the two older coaches.

Because Howard was a small college, every coach was involved in almost every aspect of the team's development, which gave Bowden an unrivaled opportunity to learn about every position on the team—how they must work together to be successful—as well as the intricate details of coaching football in general.

Toward the end of the 1954 school year, Coach Gartman decided to accept a position at another college. At about the same time, the other assistant coach decided to retire. Before Gartman made his intentions officially known to anyone else, he told Bowden he was going to recommend him for the head coach position. Since there were no other members of the coaching staff remaining, Bowden was optimistic he would get the job, but he was shocked and upset when the school's president decided not to give him the job because of his age and lack of experience. Even after he tried to convince the president that he was capable of handling the job, the president wouldn't reconsider.

Unbeknownst to Bowden, part of God's plan was about to reveal itself, and he was about to undergo another major adjustment.

It wasn't long after he was turned down for the position at Howard College that he received an unsolicited letter from President William S. Smith at South Georgia College offering him the head coaching position at SGC. When Bowden received the letter, he didn't know anything about South Georgia or its football program or even why Smith had contacted him. But he was discouraged by his situation at Howard, which he didn't expect to improve anytime in the near future, so he called Smith and accepted his offer.

Bowden accepted the offer on blind faith; he knew very little, if anything, about South Georgia. Even after he talked to Smith on the telephone, the only things he knew for sure were that he would be the head coach and athletic director, that the school had athletic scholarships, and that his starting salary would be $4,200 a year, which was about fifty dollars more a month than what he was making as an assistant at Howard.

His blind leap may not have been atypical of any young man eager for a change or unhappy with his current situation, but it could have been disastrous if God had not had His hand on Bowden's shoulder.

With his acceptance of the head coaching position at South Georgia College, the legacy of Coach Bobby Bowden began to unfold.

04

BOWDEN MOVES TO SOUTH GEORGIA

Almost immediately after Bowden accepted the head coaching job at South Georgia College in the middle of the summer of 1955, he moved his family to Douglas, Georgia. It was going to be a big adjustment for him and his wife, Ann, because they had both lived all their lives in Birmingham, Alabama, a large urban area, and Douglas, at the time, was a small town with a population of fewer than ten thousand citizens. This, combined with the fact that Bowden had never been a head coach, and had only been an assistant for two years, made him and his wife apprehensive about their move.

Once in Douglas, however, their anxieties quickly disappeared. They found the people of Douglas very friendly and supportive of both them and South Georgia College. The warm and receptive staff at SGC and its beautiful campus, with its stately buildings surrounded by an abundance of tall pine trees and blooming azaleas, also helped their adjustment.

After Bowden got over his initial nervousness, everything seemed to be going pretty well as he and his family settled into their new apartment. The word "new" in this instance is only used to imply that the apartment was their new home—it was by no means a new building structurally. In fact, the building their apartment was located in was actually an old, decaying, dilapidated Army Air Corps barracks that had been used to house cadets at a flight training facility during World War II, but their rent was only $25 a month and included utilities. But, even the substandard condition of their apartment didn't discourage Bowden from being excited about his new job and what he hoped was his future in the coaching profession.

It wasn't until a short time later, when he learned more about the finer specifics of his responsibilities, that he started having second thoughts about his decision. His biggest surprise came when he found out that he was expected to be the basketball and baseball coach in addition to being the head football coach and the school's athletic director. The thought of coaching basketball in particular gave him an uncomfortable feeling.

Coaching baseball wasn't as big of a problem because he had played baseball in high school and college and knew something about it. But basketball was another story. He was positive that the only thing he really knew about basketball was that he didn't know enough about it to be the coach. The more he thought about coaching basketball, the more he questioned his decision to move to South Georgia.

Beyond his uneasiness with basketball, he also worried that he wouldn't have enough time to develop a successful football program if he had to coach basketball. And, since basketball started immediately after football season, he knew he wouldn't have time to get ready for basketball while he was coaching football. Bowden started thinking that he would be very lucky just to get through the first basketball season without completely embarrassing himself, the school, and the entire basketball team.

It also occurred to him that if he was coaching basketball, he wouldn't have time to get ready for spring football practice, which usually began right after basketball season. To make matters worse, basketball season fell in the middle of the school year—the time when most college football coaches were out recruiting players. If he was coaching basketball, he wouldn't be able to do any recruiting, and since he believed that recruiting was one of the most important aspects of developing a successful football program, he felt that coaching basketball would surely jeopardize any success he had hoped to achieve as South Georgia's football coach.

Before he was able to decide how to deal with basketball, he was faced with another disappointment. He discovered that South Georgia's limited budget only allowed for eighteen athletic scholarships, and that these eighteen scholarships were divided between the football, basketball, and baseball programs. Bowden knew that scholarships were essential to recruiting the best football players, and his inability to offer them fueled his frustration.

More than anything else, he was upset with himself. He knew that he shouldn't have accepted the job before he found out more about it, and he clearly recalled that when he talked to President Smith on the telephone before taking the job, he specifically asked about scholarships for football players, and Smith had said there was "some money available for some scholarships." He'd said *some* money for *some* scholarships, but he'd never said how much money or how many scholarships. Bowden had wanted to believe there were plenty of scholarships because he was unhappy with his situation at Howard.

Bowden believed his ability to be a successful football coach at South Georgia would be hindered because of the scholarship situation. It didn't matter how he looked at his additional responsibilities, especially basketball, he couldn't see them as anything but impediments that would eventually reflect poorly on him and his coaching career.

These disappointments, mixed with the euphoria of being a head football coach and athletic director at such a young age, put him under a lot of emotional strain, which started affecting his personal life. He began to wonder whether he was really doing what God expected him to be doing, or doing what he wanted to do.

After wrestling with his doubts for a few days, he finally decided that he needed to get back to handling his decisions the way he had been taught by his mother when he was a young boy: prayerfully seeking God's will.

As soon as he asked God for guidance, he saw that his concerns were never as monumental as he first thought. He realized every profession had disappointments and obstacles to overcome, but if a person really wanted to succeed, he had to stay focused and continue working toward the greater goal. In his case, that greater goal was first and foremost to serve God. After that, his outlook changed, and he started working with a positive attitude. Since then, he has lived and worked by this standard.

After Bowden accepted the reality of his new responsibilities, he concentrated on South Georgia's 1955 football season and their first game, which was scheduled for October 1. Only eight weeks until the opening game and he still had to develop a football program, put together a team, and, hopefully, do some recruiting before starting preseason practice in September.

Knowing he had a lot to accomplish, Bowden decided to talk to President Smith about the scholarship program first. When he expressed his concerns about the scarcity of scholarships available for football players, Smith suggested—since he felt so strongly—that he should try to raise some money on his own. Smith said if he was successful, the money could be used to supplement what was already in the scholarship fund. Finally, Smith informed him that since he was the athletic director, he had the authority and could use his own discretion when deciding how scholarship money would be divided between the various athletic programs.

When Bowden left the president's office, he was so excited about raising money for scholarships that he immediately started canvassing every merchant in the Douglas area asking for contributions to South Georgia's athletics scholarship fund.

With his friendly demeanor and natural enthusiasm, and because most of the merchants in this small community had always tried to support South Georgia College, it didn't take him long to raise about $3,000 to add to the school's hope chest. The school's tuition at the time was about $45 per quarter (the school operated on the quarter system instead of the semester system), and the cost for room and board was an additional $110. Considering that $155 would pay the cost for a student to attend South Georgia for one quarter, and $465 would pay for an entire year, $3,000 was a big boost to their scholarship program.

Bowden was pleased with the influx of scholarship funds, but he couldn't stop wondering whether there was enough time left before the season started for these funds to benefit the 1955 team. Even with the extra money, he had little or no time to spend recruiting. And even if he had time, he didn't have any experience; besides, he wasn't sure that any football player who hadn't already committed himself to another school would want to come to South Georgia.

When Coach Mrvos, Bowden's only assistant, returned to South Georgia from summer leave, they talked about how many players Mrvos thought might be returning from the 1954 team. Mrvos, who had also been Coach Joe Davis's assistant in 1954, knew more about the previous year's football team and its players than anyone else at South Georgia. Unfortunately, the talk did little to ease Bowden's mind; Mrvos said they shouldn't expect more than eight or nine players to come back for the 1955 season.

This dismal outlook quickly negated any excitement he had felt about extra scholarship money. Even with the extra money, he wasn't sure there would be any players around to offer a scholarship to.

While he was getting acclimated to his new pressure cooker environment and trying to figure out how he was going to get enough players to field a team in 1955, Bowden learned a lot more about the history of football at South Georgia College. The information not only provided him with some history of South Georgia, it gave him some much-needed relief and encouragement.

He discovered that with few exceptions, South Georgia had always had a strong football team that had historically attracted a large number of players—even though there had never been much of a recruiting program or effort. And no one he talked to could see any reason why

1955 would be any different from previous years.

South Georgia's solid reputation for developing outstanding football teams and players inspired many recent high school graduates to want to play football at South Georgia, even though they were never actively recruited. It seemed these young men were inspired mainly by South Georgia's football history and the fact that many of its players had gone on to very successful playing careers at larger universities after completing two years at South Georgia. Many were even willing to play without any financial aid.

In addition, a few young men came to South Georgia to play football after they had been advised by a coach or recruiter at a larger four-year college that they needed an extra year or two to mature, and maybe grow some, while honing their football skills. Very often these same coaches and recruiters would recommend South Georgia because of its proven record of developing outstanding players. It was well known that the universities of Georgia and Florida often used South Georgia as a preparatory school for future players.

It wasn't unusual for a few young men just completing high school to try out for the football team at SGC after realizing on their own that they needed some extra experience before trying to make a team at a larger university. Neither was it uncommon for a number of recently graduated high school players to show up at South Georgia's preseason camp simply because they had not been recruited by another college or university. For them, South Georgia was a proving ground.

In addition, almost every year, several men recently released from military service came to South Georgia to try out for the football team. Most of these veterans played high school ball but, for various reasons, went directly into military service after graduating instead of attempting to continue playing at some college or university. Once out of the military, they began to think about playing football again, and a junior college was their most logical choice.

These veterans, as a general rule, were more mature than most young men just graduating from high school, and because of their maturity, they were highly valued. A few even played football on a service team while in the military, bringing a wealth of playing experience with them when they came to South Georgia.

Almost all of the veterans attended college on the GI Bill, and their government assistance generally paid all of their expenses, which meant that a scholarship wasn't always their biggest concern.

South Georgia also got a few players from larger colleges or universities who would transfer to South Georgia because they were having academic problems or they'd been injured and relegated to a lower position on the team. Some were simply unhappy with their situations at the larger institutions, and some just wanted to be closer to home.

Once Bowden had time to digest this information, he realized he could probably expect a large number of eager prospects—possessing various levels of experience and athletic skills—to show up for preseason camp as soon as he announced the starting date.

05
FOOTBALL BEGINS AT
SOUTH GEORGIA UNDER BOWDEN

As history predicted, on a bright, sunny Sunday afternoon at the end of the first week of September in 1955, approximately sixty eager young men showed up at South Georgia's gymnasium to meet Coaches Bowden and Mrvos and get ready for a new football season.

The candidates were issued uniforms and assigned a room in either Proctor or Powell Hall—two of the dormitories that would be used by the 1955 football team. They were also instructed to be ready to start their first practice the next morning at six thirty. For the next two weeks they would practice twice a day: six thirty in the morning and four o'clock in the afternoon.

Their first week of practices started one week prior to freshmen orientation—freshmen were required to attend a daily two-hour orientation for a week—and two weeks prior to the official start of the quarter. Its timing was selected so that every player would have at least two weeks to concentrate as much as possible on football, to learn Bowden's coaching methods and expectations, and to make the Tigers' football team.

Of those that showed up for camp, all but eight were freshmen. The eight who were not freshmen played on the Tigers' 1954 team and included two running backs and six linemen. The two running backs were Ronnie Kelley, a halfback from Griffin, Georgia, who was also the team's leading ground gainer in 1954, and Billy Thornton, another halfback from Columbus, Georgia. The six linemen were Bobby Keys, a guard from Ringgold, Georgia, who was voted lineman of the year by his teammates in 1954; Monty Roberts, an end from Griffin, Georgia; Mitchell "Ape" Adams, a guard from Commerce, Georgia; Milton "Reverend" Cooper, a guard from Jacksonville, Florida; William "Barrel" Wilson, a guard from Commerce, Georgia; and Richard Johnson, an end from Elberton, Georgia.

Kelley and Keys were the only two players in this group promised any financial assistance from the school, and that promise was made prior to Bowden's hiring. None of the other players had been, or would be, promised any assistance until the end of the second week. Bowden had decided he wanted to wait until then before he discussed this phase of his program with any player. He planned to end their first week of practice with a game-type scrimmage, which he and Coach Mrvos agreed would give them the best opportunity to evaluate the players before offering financial aid.

With only eight players back from the 1954 team, it was obvious that Mrvos' prediction of having to depend largely on freshmen to make up their 1955 squad had been accurate.

Fortunately for the Tigers, a large number of the fifty-plus freshmen were recently discharged military veterans. As had also been predicted, some of these veterans actually played football while serving. Some of those who didn't have the opportunity to play while in the military were directly involved in combat in the Korean conflict.

The two most important things about this group of veterans, in Bowden's opinion, were that they were all older and more mature than typical freshman and they were all attending college on the GI Bill, which paid their tuition, their room and board, and gave them a small stipend for additional expenses.

Bowden believed that when he started offering scholarships, because of the limited number available, he had to consider every-thing if he wanted to balance the needs of the team with the needs of the players and gain the greatest benefit for both.

❖ ❖ ❖

EVEN THOUGH THIS WAS BOWDEN'S first year as a head coach, he was experienced enough as a player and an assistant coach to know that the first couple weeks of practice were always the toughest part of the entire football season, both physically and mentally, for everyone involved. Some players would be eliminated because they were unwilling to "pay the price" necessary to make the team.

In the 1950s, players had to be conditioned to play an entire game on both sides of the football (offensively and defensively), and in many cases, without a break. There was no such thing as a player who specialized in just one or two aspects of the game, such as a kicker, or someone who played only offense or defense. There were no special teams. It was an era when young men played football because they loved the game, they loved competition, and they loved being part of a team and associating with their teammates.

It was also a time when free substitution, or anything similar to it, wasn't allowed. No player or group of players could enter or leave the game just because he or the coaches wanted to make a change. The rules on substitution at that time stated that any player who started a game, or quarter during the game, could come out and reenter the game only one time during the same quarter. If he came out a second time during that same quarter, he was not allowed to reenter until the next quarter. Any player who didn't start the game or a particular quarter, but entered as a substitute during a quarter, could not come out and reenter the game during the same quarter. If he came out for any reason, he had to stay out until the next quarter.

Because of these restrictions, a player who was only interested in specializing in a certain aspect of the game was not the type of player that any coach looked for while putting together a team. The players coaches wanted and needed were those who were willing to be conditioned to play the entire game and sometimes to play even when hurt. Therefore, conditioning players was critical and a top priority for most coaches. As a result, most coaches designed and planned their practices to last two to three hours without a break. During the early part of the season, it was not unusual for these practices to be conducted in steaming hot temperatures without breaks to rest or rehydrate. Most coaches thought that if a player drank anything when he was hot and sweaty, his muscles would cramp; therefore, drinking anything during practice was prohibited.

Occasionally, when the temperature was really hot, Bowden would allow one of the team managers to go around during practice with a wet towel and wipe the dirt and sweat off the players' faces. It wasn't uncommon for some players who were really suffering to grab the towel and try to suck the water out of it.

Practice was conducted in full uniform and ended with fifty- or one-hundred-yard wind sprints. These sprints, often referred to as "gassers," lasted until most of the players were gasping for breath and a few were regurgitating. It was not unusual for players to be on their hands and knees, completely exhausted, when the gassers were completed.

Today this may seem a little harsh to some, but in the '50s it was typical, and most coaches and players accepted this type of conditioning, believing it was necessary. Even Bowden and Mrvos, who were always concerned about the health and well-being of their players, accepted this philosophy. They had experienced the same type of conditioning when they were players, and they expected no less of their team.

When Bowden is asked to compare today's players with those who played for him when he first started coaching, he frequently says, "Today's players are a lot bigger and faster, but they are not nearly as tough as players were when I first started coaching. Today, when you tell a player to do something, you'll have to explain to him why. When I first started coaching, you could tell a player to run head first into a brick wall, and before you got the last word out of your mouth, he was already running toward the wall with his head down…Yup, players in the 1950s were not as smart as players are today, but they were a lot tougher."

Bowden has said that the majority of players in the 1950s were so tough that they didn't know the meaning of fear. After some thought, he's been known to smile and add, "In all honesty, those same players probably didn't know the meaning of a lot of words."

At the conclusion of the first week of practice, things were going pretty much as Bowden and Mrvos had anticipated. A few players had already quit, apparently deciding to seek their fame at some other school or in some other arena, while others were beginning to stand out. The first scrimmage, as expected, gave both coaches a better idea of where the team's strengths and weaknesses were and where they needed to concentrate their building efforts. It also gave them a better feel for which of the returning lettermen, as well as the new players, they could depend on.

No one was surprised when Ronnie Kelley and Bobby Keys picked up from where they left off the previous year and were recognized as team leaders. For that reason, Bowden appointed them team captains for the 1955 season.

By the end of the second week, both coaches had already identified the freshmen they believed were performing well enough to make the team and the players they thought should get scholarships. Once the decision was made, Bowden spoke privately with those selected and told them the amount of assistance they would receive, which ranged anywhere from $60 a quarter to a full scholarship that would pay for tuition and room and board.

When all the scholarships were awarded, Bowden talked to the players who were not selected, and he explained to them how he made his decisions. In most cases, he encouraged them to stay on the team, explaining that things could always change in the future. Most of the players who didn't receive any financial assistance appreciated Bowden's honesty and decided to remain with the team. A few, however, obviously disappointed, turned in their uniforms.

After all was said and done, the team was comprised of almost forty players, and those who were starting lineup material were beginning to emerge.

Once the team was complete, Bowden extended an invitation to all of the players, which became one of the hallmarks of his tenure at South Georgia. That invitation usually went something like this: "The pastor at the First Baptist Church in Douglas has invited all of us to attend their Sunday morning service. Since I believe that it would be beneficial to all of us to accept his invitation, I plan on being there, and I hope some of you will also. If transportation is a problem, let me know and I'll make arrangements for anyone who needs a ride."

Many players didn't hesitate to respond to Bowden's suggestion. Later, they began to attend church regularly. A few, on the other hand, who were at first reluctant, went only because they thought Bowden would think less of them if they didn't, which he never did. But after they started attending and saw how serious Bowden was about his faith—always sitting in the front of the church and listening very attentively to the pastor's message—their attitude began to change and the services began to have more of an impact on their lives.

The 1955 South Georgia football squad was made up of the following 36 members:

NAMES	POSITION	WEIGHT	NUMBER
Mitchell "Ape" Adams	Guard	195	32
Malcolm Ayers	End	176	22
Jerome "Blinkey" Barber	Fullback	180	16
Vernon Brinson	Halfback	155	23
Bruce Childs	End	168	29
Milton "Reverend" Cooper	Guard	180	41
Jimmy "Fats" DePalma	Tackle	215	50
Bobby Dixon	Fullback	180	19
Gene "Doolebug" Edwards	Halfback	165	15
Billy "Stumpy" Franklin	Guard	195	33
James Gardner	End	175	38
Everett Graham	Halfback	170	31

Charles Gulbrandsen	Tackle	225	42
Mike Hampton	Quarterback	170	5
Billy Hayes	Tackle	200	25
Jerry Holland	Center	195	30
Richard Johnson	End	205	61
Jack Kicklighter	Guard	190	52
Ronnie Kelley	Halfback	160	10
Bobby Keys	Guard	196	26
Fred Levy	Guard	190	11
Freddy Mincey	Center	187	71
Cecil Morris	Tackle	210	85
Rosby Mulkey	Tackle	230	70
Judon Parker	Center	205	40
Gene Phillips	Halfback	192	73
Monty Roberts	End	187	51
Leeon "Bull" Smith	End	190	13
Hoke Smith	End	196	39
Raymond South	Guard/Tackle	185	36
Bobby Sowell	End	180	35
Homer Sowell	End	205	83
Louis Studdard	Quarterback	195	14
Billy Thornton	Halfback	166	9
Roger Wilkinson	Quarterback	180	12
Lynford Wood	Tackle	215	72

Once the final selections were made, the team had less than a week to get ready for their first game against Middle Georgia College on October 1, in Cochran, Georgia.

On Thursday, September 29, shortly after their final full-contact drill, Bowden announced the Tigers' starting lineup—except for two positions that were still in question due to injuries. The most critical of the two questionable positions, and the one that concerned Bowden the most, was the quarterback position. Louis Studdard was initially expected to start at quarterback, but because of a recent wrist injury Bowden wasn't sure he would be able to play.

If Studdard was unable to play, the team would have to depend almost entirely on Roger Wilkinson, but Wilkinson had never played a game at quarterback before. He'd come to SGC as a running back, but during the first week of practice, Bowden moved him to quarterback to add more depth to this position.

If Wilkinson had to start their first game, he would be expected to play almost every play on offense at quarterback and almost every play on defense as a defensive back or linebacker. If he got injured, or for some other reason was unable to complete the game, the Tigers and Bowden would be left in a very precarious situation.

Ready or not, on October 1, when kickoff time arrived, the following players were slated to start for the Tigers:

Center	Judon Parker	Freshman
Guard	Mitchell Adams	Sophomore
Guard	Bobby Keys	Sophomore
Tackle	Charles Gulbrandsen	Freshman
Tackle	Rosby Mulkey	Freshman
End	Homer Sowell	Freshman
End	Monty Roberts	Sophomore
Quarterback	Roger Wilkinson	Freshman
Halfback	Ronnie Kelley	Sophomore
Halfback	Everett Graham	Freshman
Fullback	Jerome Barber	Freshman

This lineup included four sophomores and seven untried freshmen, including Wilkinson, who would have the enormous task, as well as the dubious distinction, of leading a team prepared by a coach who himself had never been tested as a head coach.

06

A REAL LEARNING EXPERIENCE:
THE FIRST HALF OF THE 1955 SEASON

South Georgia Tigers vs Middle Georgia Wolverines

On *October* 1, the South Georgia Tigers made the 120-mile trek to Cochran, Georgia, to play the Middle Georgia Wolverines. It was the first game of the season, and everyone on the team was more anxious than normal.

It's not unusual for athletes to get a little more nervous than usual before the first game of a new season, but the 1955 South Georgia squad had to play their first game with seven untested freshmen in their starting lineup, including a quarterback who had never played the position before, and a new head coach who was coaching his baptismal game. And, they didn't even have home-field advantage. Even today, after more than fifty years in the coaching profession, Bowden admits that his nervousness before that game has never been equaled.

One player described that edgy bus ride saying, "If all the butterflies churning in our stomachs before that game could have been gathered up and inserted into the stomach of just one player, that person would have made Elvis Presley's gyrations when he sang 'All Shook Up' look like a slow waltz."

Fortunately for the Tigers, once the game got underway, their stomachs settled down and they took control of the game and never let up until the final whistle blew.

Using a powerful running attack led by Roger Wilkinson, their previously untested quarterback, they ran over and through the Wolverines' defense, scoring at least one touchdown every quarter.

They picked up 15 first downs, rushed for 332 yards, and scored 32 points, compared to the Wolverines' 6 first downs, 42 yards rushing, and 12 points.

To everyone's surprise, Wilkinson played with such finesse and confidence that no one on their opponent's team ever guessed that he wasn't a seasoned field general. He solidified his starting role in the fourth quarter when he raced 53 yards to score their final touchdown.

Halfback Ronnie Kelley and fullback Bobby Dixon divided the remaining four touchdowns. When the final whistle blew, Bowden was as much relieved to finally get his maiden game behind him as he was excited about their win. He told the media he was especially pleased with the way the offense had moved the football so effectively on the ground, and in addition to praising Wilkinson, he commended all of the starting linemen for their outstanding yeoman duty. "It was the play of our linemen and the way they consistently opened holes in the Wolverines' defense that made the difference in the game," he said.

Once the Tigers had their first victory securely tucked under their helmets, Bowden and the entire team felt a lot more confident about the remainder of the season.

Several veteran Tigers said it was easy to see a big improvement in the team's overall performance from the previous season. Ape Adams, one of their starting guards, said that Coach Bowden did an outstanding job getting them ready for the game. He described Bowden as the most organized coach he had ever seen or played for, adding that he had organized every practice session down to the last minute. Ronnie Kelley, a running back and one of the team's captains, stated that Bowden's positive attitude and obvious respect for his players made it easy for them to develop a winning spirit.

The Tigers' season-opening victory helped propel them into their first home game at South Georgia's College Field against the West Georgia College Braves the next Saturday night.

South Georgia Tigers vs West Georgia Braves

SOUTH GEORGIA'S GAME AGAINST THE WEST GEORGIA BRAVES, ON October 7, started out as a defensive battle between two strong, equally determined football teams. Because of their offense's success the week before, Bowden was surprised that they had hit a stone wall and were having so much trouble moving the football.

After a couple of exchanged punts, however, the Tigers' linemen finally gained control of the line of scrimmage, and with this domination, their running backs found a few weak seams in their opponents' defense, which allowed them to move the football with a lot more consistency in the latter part of the first quarter.

The key that unlocked the stalemate was a 25-yard sprint by Ronnie Kelley to the Braves' 28-yard line after he grabbed a short swing pass from Wilkinson. Everett Graham and Blinkey Barber moved the ball to the 6-yard line before Kelley brought the drive to its conclusion when he charged into pay dirt for the game's first touchdown.

After scoring, the Tigers' linemen demonstrated why Bowden considered them the backbone of this team. Led by guard Bobby Keys and tackle Rosby Mulkey, they held the Braves' offense to short, insignificant gains every time they had possession of the football.

On offense, Wilkinson mixed running and passing plays for a more balanced offense, which kept the Braves' defense confused enough for the Tigers to score two more touchdowns before the first half ended. By then the Tigers were comfortably ahead by 19 points.

Immediately after the second half got underway, the Braves received the kickoff and put together their best drive of the contest, scoring their first and only 6-pointer.

With the scoreboard reflecting the Tigers' 13-point lead, the game turned back into a punting contest for the remainder of the third quarter.

Once the fourth quarter started, the Tigers went back to playing with the same intensity they'd demonstrated in the first half. They put together a slow, methodical 80-yard drive that included a sizzling 16-yard pass from Wilkinson to Vernon Brinson, and Brinson's subsequent 12-yard dash that paid off when Graham bolted into the end zone, scoring their fourth and final touchdown.

This final TD gave the South Georgian's a well-deserved 25-6 victory.

With the exception of the third period, the Tigers dominated the game—rushing for a total of 322 yards, passing for 116 yards, and picking up 20 first downs, which made the Braves' 82 yards rushing, 106 yards passing, and 6 first downs look a little shabby.

Bowden commented after the game that it was, again, the play of their linemen that made the difference in the outcome of the game. In particular, he praised Charles Gulbrandsen, Bobby Keys, Ape Adams, Rosby Mulkey, Monty Roberts, and Homer Sowell.

This second win, especially since they defeated another important conference rival, reinforced the team's hopes of winning the Georgia State Junior College Conference Championship, and it made the excitement around SGC's campus something to behold for the next few days.

No one at South Georgia doubted the Tigers would win their next game against Jones County Junior College in Ellisville, Mississippi, the following weekend.

After two decisive victories, Bowden felt like he pretty much had coaching football down to a science, or at least, he had it down well enough to control his team's destiny in most games. Of course, he admits now that his assumption was misguided by his inexperience and youthful enthusiasm— it was a very painful experience when the bubble burst the very next weekend against Jones County.

That game, he remembers, reintroduced him to the harsh reality and true complexities of this game called football. It also reminded him of an important truism that he, and everyone else associated with the Tigers' football team, had forgotten: the simple truth is that no football team or football coach has a patent on winning any football game. This truism is now firmly etched in his memory, and he relies on it to guide him when he prepares any of his teams for a game.

South Georgia Tigers vs Jones County Bobcats

THE TIGERS' GAME against the Jones County Bobcats was scheduled for October 15 in Ellisville, Mississippi, and it would be their third game of the season.

In October of 1955, the Williamson Rating Board, which ranked and rated junior college football teams nationwide in the 1950s, had ranked Jones County Junior College fourth nationally.

South Georgia, who had won their first two games convincingly, was not even ranked in the top twenty-five teams, which was understandable because the criterion used by the Williamson Rating Board in the first part of any season was based largely on a team's previous year's performance. And, of course, South Georgia's 1954 season wasn't anything anyone was bragging about. (NOTE: At the end of the 1955 season, Jones County was ranked second nationally behind Compton Junior College from Compton, California. Compton College earned the top slot by narrowly defeating Jones County in the Little Rose Bowl at season's end).

Prior to their game in Mississippi, neither Bowden nor anyone on the Tigers' team knew very much about the Bobcats and nothing about their national ranking. If they knew anything at all, it was only because Bowden had talked on the telephone briefly with the Bobcat's coach earlier in the week and the two of them exchanged some nonessential information about their teams.

Going into their game against the Bobcats, the Tigers felt they could compete with any junior college team in the nation and probably some four-year colleges too. Their confidence made them eager to get to Mississippi and play the game, anticipating another victory.

Their trip from South Georgia to Ellisville, Mississippi, was over four hundred miles, and Bowden expected it to take about thirteen or fourteen hours. They would be traveling in an old flat-nose school bus, referred to by all of the players as the "Blue Goose." The bus was equipped with hard bench seats, typical of school buses in the 1950s, and there were no interstate highways existing at the time, so the entire trip would be on two-lane highways. Everyone on the team knew the trip would be long and physically exhausting, but that didn't dampen their excitement or enthusiasm.

They left SGC before daylight Friday morning, October 14, and expected to arrive in Ellisville around eight or nine o'clock that evening. During the trip, some of the players would lie down on their bags stacked in the rear of the bus and try to get some rest. Others attempted to ward off boredom playing cards in the aisle or reading. Sleeping in a seat was impossible unless one could sleep sitting straight up with nothing to rest his head on.

A couple of players who had vehicles were allowed to drive to Ellisville in convoy with the bus, and a few of their teammates rode with them.

Prior to leaving Douglas, Bowden directed the bus driver to plan their trip so they would go through Troy, Alabama. Bowden was always trying to think ahead, and since they were scheduled to play Troy State Teacher's College the following weekend but didn't have the funds to pay a staff member to scout a future opponent, he devised a plan he thought would overcome the monetary shortfall.

He planned to leave Coach Mrvos—his only assistant—at a motel somewhere along the highway close to Troy's campus. The next evening, while they were in Mississippi playing Jones County, Mrvos would be in Troy scouting the Trojans, their next opponent. Sunday afternoon, they would pick Mrvos up at the same location when they passed back through Troy on their way home.

The plan seemed like a good idea at the time, but in reality, it left the Tigers with only one coach on the sideline while facing what turned out to be their toughest junior college opponent of the year.

When they finally arrived in Ellisville that evening, it was late at night and Bowden instructed all of his players to go to bed and try to get a good night's sleep. Their host's athletic department had arranged to have folding cots set up in the school's gym to accommodate them. Several South Georgia players clearly recall that not only were those cots uncomfortable and hard to sleep on, but their host—they are now convinced—conveniently forgot to heat the water for the showers.

The next morning, Bowden did what he later recalled was the dumbest thing he has ever done to get a team ready to play a football game. He got the entire team up for an early breakfast. After they finished eating breakfast, he sent them back to bed for more rest. If they couldn't sleep, he instructed them to just lie quietly on their cots and conserve their energy.

Around midday, he got everyone back up for lunch. When they finished lunch, he ordered them back to bed, thinking they needed all the rest they could get after their long trip.

Today, he remorsefully remembers that his overzealous effort to rest his team was a huge mistake. Shortly after the game started, he realized his players were so "dadgum rested" they could barely move, much less run.

On the game's opening kickoff, Jones County fumbled the football deep inside their own territory, where the Tigers recovered it. This should have been a golden opportunity for the Tigers, but the Tigers responded by fumbling the ball right back to the Bobcats on the first play from scrimmage.

After their initial fumble, the Bobcats ran over, around, and through the Tigers like a herd of wild horses, while the Tigers limped around stiff, numb, and half-dazed. That's when it really hit Bowden that too much rest after a long bus ride wasn't the best way to get ready for a football game.

Those who remember that game remember a very embarrassing, painful experience.

During the first half, the Tigers couldn't get their defense organized, and, when on offense, they couldn't find the handle on the football. Consequently, their defense was never able to stop the Bobcats' assault, and the offense did nothing but turn the football over to the Bobcats. In fact, just about every time the Tigers had possession of the football, they either fumbled it or threw an interception.

The Bobcats scored at will, and by the end of the first half they had scored 5 touchdowns and were leading the bewildered and embarrassed Tigers by 33 points.

The Tigers' locker room was like a morgue at halftime. Bowden was so embarrassed and dispirited he could hardly talk. There were no rallying speeches like those he has since become famous for; all he could muster was a plea to hold onto the football if they ever got it again.

Despite the lack of a pep talk, the Tigers took the second half's opening kickoff and initiated their best offensive drive of the game. In this drive they not only held onto the football, they moved it farther into the Bobcats' end of the field than they had been able to at any time during the first half. They even threatened to score. Suddenly they were playing like they realized they were in the middle of a football game.

Their offense wasn't the only part of their game that came alive either. After they were stopped just short of the goal line and forced to give the ball back to the Bobcats, their defense played like a completely different team. They held the Bobcats' offense to almost no gain and forced them to punt after three plays.

After the Bobcats' punted and the Tigers regained possession of the ball, they put together another determined and impressive offensive march. Starting from their own 40-yard line, they quickly moved the ball to their opponent's 43-yard line before Wilkinson went to the airwaves and unleashed a beautiful 36-yard pass to Homer Sowell. Wilkinson's connection with Sowell put them on the 7-yard line, and from there, Ronnie Kelley hauled the pigskin to the 1-foot line. Once they reached the 1-foot line, Wilkinson dove over the line of scrimmage into the end zone, scoring their first TD.

That touchdown and the team's newfound enthusiasm let Bowden hope that things were turning around and that the Tigers would begin to play as he had expected them to play. It seemed like they had taken the game's momentum away from the once-dominating Bobcats.

His hope, however, was short-lived. Once the Tigers kicked off, the Bobcats came racing back and scored their sixth touchdown.

Leading now by a score of 39-6, the Bobcats kicked off to the Tigers for the seventh time. Unlike their first six kickoffs, the ball slid off the side of their kicker's foot and barely bounced across the 50-yard line. This miscued kick gave Monty Roberts, who was lined up on the Tigers' 40-yard line, a chance to grab the short kick and fight his way back almost 26 yards to the Bobcats' 34-yard line. On the same play, the game's officials assessed a 15-yard penalty against Jones County, and the ball was moved to the Bobcats' 19-yard line. Suddenly, the Tigers were in striking distance of the goal for the third time since the second half got underway.

From the 20-yard line, Bobby Dixon charged through the Bobcats' forward wall and bolted into their secondary, picking up another 10 yards. With another first down and four plays to get into pay dirt, Louis Studdard, who had replaced Wilkinson at quarterback, flipped a short swing pass to Kelley, and Kelley high-stepped it to the 3-yard line. Billy Thornton brought the drive to a successful conclusion when he sprinted into the end zone, scoring their second touchdown. Homer Sowell converted the extra point, and South Georgia suddenly seemed to be coming alive.

But then, just when it seemed like they were getting started, their unexplainable burst of energy evaporated as mysteriously as it had appeared. Once the fourth quarter started, they went right back to playing the same laconic, uninspired football they'd played in the first two quarters.

That's when the Bobcats took complete control of the game and scored 3 more touchdowns before the final whistle blew. By then the Tigers were behind by a score of 60-13. They turned the football over to the Bobcats a total of thirteen times, seven times because of fumbles and six times due to interceptions. They also let the Bobcats capitalize on almost every turnover and score a total of nine touchdowns.

Except for the third quarter, the Tigers were never able to play competitively with the Bobcats, and in Bowden's mind, the game was a humiliating disaster.

The next day, on the trip back to Douglas, Bowden and the team were still in shock. Most of the time, the silence on the bus was deafening. The trip lasted more than thirteen hours, but there was very little, if any, talking—mostly Bowden and his players just sat quietly and stared out the bus windows.

Bowden was more disheartened than anyone, and several times he even tried to take full responsibility for the loss. In his heart and mind, he was ultimately responsible because he was the head coach.

Today, he describes that game as the most emotionally painful defeat of his entire coaching career. He has said it was the game that taught him the enormousness of a head coach's responsibilities.

The loss had him wondering again whether he was actually doing what he should be doing with his life. Had it not been for his strong convictions and his belief that it would have been unconscionable for him to quit coaching until after he had done everything in his power to help his players get past their humiliation, he could very easily have been driven out of coaching.

Bowden wrote in the preface of one of his latest books, *The Bowden Way*, which was coauthored with his oldest son, Steve Bowden, that "Football has been a great teacher. It thrust me into leadership before I felt ready to lead. It proved a harsh taskmaster at times—testing my convictions, punishing my mistakes, and relentlessly pushing me beyond myself. But it also taught me more about leadership than I could have ever gleaned from books."

Bowden was just a freshman in the head football coaching profession in 1955, but he found himself wading deep into the psychology and philosophy of the game, forcing him to learn and adapt quickly.

He knew his first undertaking had to be rebuilding his players' spirits, an enormous task, especially because their next two games were scheduled against four-year colleges with strong football programs. He visualized David facing Goliath, so he dug deep, looking for some kind of inner strength that would help him and his players prevail and avoid another humiliation.

At the first practice after their loss to Jones County, morale was as low as it could get. Without any genuine enthusiasm, the Tigers drug themselves through every drill like their pride and spirit had been totally destroyed. Seeing this, Bowden knew his most important responsibility, at least for the immediate future, was to concentrate on rebuilding their confidence and spirit. He believed restoring their spirit had to take precedence over physical conditioning, teaching football skills, and developing strategies. He was concerned that another defeat could cause his team to develop a loser's mentality, which, in his opinion, would have a devastatingly negative effect on them as a team for the rest of the season and as individuals for the rest of their lives. Another loss like the one in Jones County couldn't do anything but hurt them.

Being an eternal optimist, he thought if they were lucky enough to avoid another demeaning loss to either of their next two opponents, he might be able to get his players back to normal before the end of the season.

At every practice after that he concentrated on raising his team's spirit by staying upbeat and instilling in them the feeling that they were just as good and just as talented as any team. He repeatedly told them that if he and Coach Mrvos did their jobs, they could win most of the games left on their schedule.

By week's end, after a tough and challenging week, Bowden was as surprised as anyone when he noticed some confidence creeping back into his team. Some players even seemed to be looking forward to their next game, which helped ease some of his own anxieties.

South Georgia Tigers vs Troy State Trojans

ON FRIDAY, OCTOBER 21, Bowden and his team left Douglas for Troy, Alabama.

Their trip to Troy was another grueling ride that lasted about six hours and took them over the same route they had traveled the week before. Bowden thought the repetition might upset his players, but their eagerness didn't diminish and no one appeared to stop looking forward to the game—even though they knew they would be playing against a much larger and more experienced team.

When they finally arrived in Troy that afternoon, there was still enough time left in the day to work out some of the kinks the six-hour trip on the Blue Goose had created.

The next day, October 22, they still had plenty of time to relax and stay loose before the game. Bowden restrained himself from giving anyone any specific instructions about resting, and he never once ordered anyone confined to his bed—he'd learned his lesson after last week's game.

That evening when the Tigers and the Trojans hit the field to warm up, Bowden couldn't help but notice that his team was considerably outnumbered. Troy had approximately sixty players suited up for the game compared to South Georgia's thirty-two. David and Goliath loomed large in his imagination. He hoped the disparity didn't intimidate his players.

Once the game got underway though, he saw his team playing with the boldness and purposefulness of a vicious saber-toothed tiger fighting for its very survival. If any of his players were intimidated, it certainly wasn't apparent. If anything, it seemed that his Tigers were repeatedly knocking the larger Trojans on their keesters, making Troy struggle to compete with them.

Even after Troy managed to score first, South Georgia came storming back in the latter part of the second quarter when Gene Phillips, one of their defensive backs, intercepted a pass and returned it to the Trojans' 23-yard line. On their first play from scrimmage after the interception, Bobby Dixon charged through the line and refused to be stopped until he reached the 11-yard line. Ronnie Kelley circled around the Trojans' right end and scrambled to the 2-yard line. From the 2, Roger Wilkinson faked a lateral to Kelly and raced off-tackle for the touchdown. Homer Sowell converted the PAT, and the score was knotted at 7-7 just before the first half ended.

When they returned to the field after halftime, the third quarter looked a lot like the first half, with both teams seemingly content to let their defenses control the game. The tug-of-war lasted until Troy finally broke the tie with a touchdown. No more points were scored in the third quarter, but it was obvious that the Trojans were having a tough time maintaining their 6-point lead.

Unfortunately for the Tigers, when the final quarter got underway, the Trojans shuffled as many fresh players onto the field as possible. It wasn't long before their overwhelming bench strength took its toll on the weary South Georgia players—especially those who had been on the field since the game's opening kickoff. They had nothing left to play on but guts and pride, and as a result, Troy was able to score two more touchdowns and win the game 26-7.

Even in defeat, Bowden couldn't help being excited about the way his players had handled this senior college team, and he let it be known that they had played an outstanding game against undeniable odds. He was especially proud of Ape Adams, Charles Gulbrandsen, Rosby Mulkey, Milton Cooper, Stumpy Franklin, Cecil Morris, Fred Mincey, and Homer Sowell. "These linemen were on the field for almost the entire game, but they never quit or gave up," he said.

Speaking to a reporter from the Douglas area, he was so emotional that he kept repeating himself: "We played a much larger and more experienced team on even terms for more than three quarters, and if it hadn't been for their overwhelming numbers and their ability to keep fresh players on the field in the last quarter, we very well might have won the game."

Bowden knew they had met their Goliath, and even though they had not slain him as he had hoped, they left him shaking while they were able to walk away with renewed confidence in themselves and their team.

On their trip home, Bowden was exhilarated. In the past four months, God had allowed him to experience just about every emotional extreme possible—from the highest high to the lowest low, and he couldn't help but wonder what the future had in store for him once he got back to Georgia.

One thing he was sure of, though, was that the last few weeks had been a real learning experience that taught him more about coaching and life in general than he could have ever learned in such a short period of time under any other circumstances. It eliminated any reservations he still had as to whether he should be coaching football.

07

THE RECOVERY CONTINUES IN THE SECOND HALF OF THE SEASON

South Georgia Tigers vs Jacksonville State Gamecocks

*O*nce *South Georgia* got past their game with the Troy State Trojans, they were more eager and excited than ever to meet their next challenger: Jacksonville State Teacher's College, another four-year college team from the state of Alabama.

Bowden was happy with their enthusiasm and renewed team spirit, but he couldn't help but worry that their recovery might be coming a little too fast. He was afraid that if that was the case, any progress they had made so far would be jeopardized, and if they lost another game— or didn't play well against Jacksonville—they might fall back into an even deeper slump. He was especially worried because Jacksonville was undefeated and no team had been able to score against them in their first five games of the season.

The next Saturday night, when South Georgia and the Jacksonville Gamecocks took the field at South Georgia's College Field, Bowden's concerns multiplied when he saw the size and number of players on Jacksonville's team. Seeing the Gamecocks up close affirmed his earlier suspicions that his players were in for a rough night and about to tangle with the best team they had faced all year.

He was afraid that after his players saw the size of Jacksonville's team and players, they would lose heart, give up, and accept defeat even before the game started.

What Bowden wasn't aware of was that his players had already agreed among themselves that they weren't going to concede anything without a fight.

Even after Jacksonville scored three touchdowns early in the game, the Tigers never quit fighting. In fact, late in the second quarter they stunned everyone when they took on the role of the aggressor and scored the first touchdown any team had scored against the Gamecocks all season. The Gamecocks, in particular, were shocked that this small junior college team had scored a touchdown when no other four-year school had been able to in five games.

The Tigers' defense set up the touchdown when they stood up to the Gamecocks' offense and denied them a first down—something the Gamecocks were not used to. The Gamecocks had the football on their own 36-yard line and were facing a fourth down situation. They needed less than a yard for a first down and decided to run the ball instead of punting, apparently thinking the Tigers couldn't stop their big running backs or that they'd be able to push the smaller Tigers' defense around.

The scrappy Tigers' defense, however, had another idea, and once the dust settled, the Gamecocks discovered that instead of picking up the first down, they had actually lost yardage. Suddenly the smaller South Georgia team had taken the game's momentum and the football away from them.

The Gamecocks were more than a little surprised, which caused disarray as they clamored around the line of scrimmage trying to reorganize their defense. Roger Wilkinson, sensing their confusion, quickly handed the football off to Blinkey Barber on a straightforward fullback dive play. Once Barber got through the line of scrimmage, he lowered his head and ran over several would-be tacklers before he was finally tripped up around the 4-yard line.

That 31-yard blast accelerated the Gamecocks' demoralization, and while they were still trying to get their defense settled down, Wilkinson pitched the football to Everett Graham, who raced around his left end and into pay dirt, scoring the touchdown.

By then the Gamecocks were totally dazed. It was inconceivable to them that this junior college team would be the team to break their perfect unscored upon record. On their way to the locker room at the end of the first half, they were still shaking their heads in disbelief.

The Jacksonville coaches must have decided that because their team was having so much trouble controlling the Tigers, their best strategy when they returned to the field would be to utilize as many of their reserves as they could. Once the game resumed and the substitutions began, the South Georgian's felt the impact on the field immediately.

Bowden wasn't surprised when he saw that his team was confronted with the same situation they had faced the week before against Troy. He felt helpless, knowing they didn't have the reserve depth they needed to compete with Jacksonville's much larger numbers. As a result, the Gamecocks were able to score two more touchdowns and kick a field goal before winning the game by a score of 36-12.

Although the final score may have looked one-sided, Bowden knew it was a much closer game than the numbers indicated. He was proud of his team—they never gave up and never quit struggling even though they were hopelessly out-manned. Not only did the Tigers score the season's first touchdown against the Gamecocks, they rubbed a little more sand in their wounds in the latter part of the final quarter when Ronnie Kelley brought a beautiful 65-yard drive to a climax as he swivel-hipped his way into the end zone, scoring their second touchdown.

After the game, Tiger fans everywhere were surprised by their team's spirit and how well they had played. The Gamecocks were probably even more surprised than anyone by the determination and courage the South Georgians demonstrated—especially after the Tigers shattered their dreams of having a perfect, unscored upon season.

South Georgia Tigers vs Georgia Military Bulldogs

AFTER THEIR GAME WITH JACKSONVILLE, Bowden put the last three weeks behind him and concentrated on their next game against

Georgia Military College. The game was scheduled for November 5 at South Georgia's College Field, and would be the Tigers' first game against another junior college team since their game against Jones County. The GMC game could be the most important game remaining on their schedule, primarily because it would be their first real test against another junior college team, and it could set the tone for the rest of the season.

Understanding the importance of the game, he returned their practices to full-contact and conditioning drills. Then, after finishing a tough week of practice, he declared to a local reporter, "We're ready and I believe capable of defeating the GMC Bulldogs." Bowden's declaration was an indication of his renewed confidence in his team's ability to win.

But his confidence conflicted with the opinions of most sportswriters covering the Georgia Junior College Conference. With only one exception, every forecaster who prepared an article about the contest predicted that Georgia Military College was the better team and would win the game. The one exception was a little more cautious, saying only that the game would be a tossup between a strong Georgia Military squad, whom these writers unanimously believed had the best line in the conference, and the South Georgia Tigers, whose strength was in their offense.

On November 5, the game that had been touted as another lost cause for the Tigers got underway with the Tigers receiving the opening kickoff. Once the Tigers took possession of the ball, they seized the game's momentum and started moving up field toward the Dogs' goal line with such control that the commentators who had predicted that GMC was the better team must have been choking on the crow that the Tigers were shoveling down their throats.

Starting from their own 38-yard line, Roger Wilkinson seized an early opportunity to prove those writers dead wrong when he rolled out to his right and unleashed a long arched pass to Homer Sowell that netted 42 yards and another first down on the Bulldogs'

20-yard line. Two plays later, he struck again when he released his second aerial and hit Leeon "Bull" Smith inside the 10-yard line. In less than three minutes, the Tigers had another first down and four plays to get into the end zone.

On their next play, Blinkey Barber fought his way to the 3-yard line, then Bobby Keys and Rosy Mulley, two of the Tiger's linemen, opened a gaping hole in the Bulldogs' defense for Everett Graham to dance through for their first TD. Homer Sowell added the extra point, and six plays after the opening kickoff, the Tigers were leading 7-0.

After the Tigers jumped on the scoreboard, the game turned into a hard-fought defensive battle between two determined and seemingly equally spirited football teams for the rest of the first quarter. This standoff continued until shortly after the second quarter began when Wilkinson orchestrated a play-action option pass and pitched the ball to Graham. Once Graham tucked the ball under his arm, he galloped 62 yards to the Bulldogs' end zone for another Tiger score. But, because of a clipping penalty, the play was called back and the touchdown was nullified.

Not to be discouraged, the Tigers came right back and worked their way from their own 23-yard line to the 48-yard line. They were stalled at the 48 and faced with a fourth-down situation, needing 2 yards for a first down.

Since the score was still close and the game was only in the second quarter, the safe option, according to most skilled football practitioners in the 1950s, would have been to punt and try to move the Bulldogs back, deep inside their own territory. Knowing conventional wisdom wouldn't have escaped the Bulldogs and their coaches, Bowden directed his team to set up in a punt formation with Wilkinson in the deep punter's slot.

The Bulldogs, of course, went into a punt return formation and prepared to receive the Tigers' kick.

When the ball was snapped, however, instead of punting as

the Bulldogs expected, Wilkinson executed a perfect fake punt and threw a quick flat pass to Graham. The Bulldogs' defense was caught completely off guard, and Graham broke loose again and raced 52 yards into pay dirt for the Tigers' second TD.

The Tigers were ready to take their 13-point lead to the locker room at halftime, but the Bulldogs weren't ready to concede. They came fighting back just before the whistle sounded to end the first half and scored their own touchdown, cutting the Tigers' lead to 6 points.

At the start of the second half, the Bulldogs were still fired up, and the game's momentum seemed to have shifted to their side of the field. With their newfound enthusiasm, they wasted little time moving the football to the Tigers' 9-yard line before the sleeping Tigers woke up. Once they got inside South Georgia's red zone on their way to tying the score, Homer and Bobby Sowell, the Tigers' two defensive ends, started blitzing their quarterback.

The sudden change of tactics and the Sowell brothers' fierce assault disrupted their quarterback's rhythm so much that he hurriedly threw two incomplete passes over the back of the end zone.

Two plays later, the Tigers' defense completely shut the Bulldogs down 3 yards short of a touchdown.

The Bulldogs' failure to score after getting so close to the Tigers' end zone quickly returned the football and the game's momentum to the Tigers.

After regaining momentum, the Tigers initiated a beautiful game-controlling 97-yard march back to the Bulldogs' goal line. The slow, methodical, time-consuming drive eventually reached its conclusion when Wilkinson pushed the pigskin into the end zone behind the blocking of center Jerry Holland and guard Milton Cooper. With this score, the Tigers went ahead of the Bulldogs by 12 points.

In the fourth and final quarter, defense again dominated the game. The only score was a 17-yard field goal by Homer Sowell who split the uprights for the Tigers as the final seconds ticked off the scoreboard clock.

Sowell's field goal gave the Tigers a 22-7 victory over the Bulldogs.

The game was the Tigers' third conference win, which meant they could still win the conference trophy if they won their next two games. It also meant they had passed one of their biggest tests of the season, according to Bowden.

South Georgia Tigers vs Middle Georgia Wolverines

As HAPPY AS BOWDEN was about the win against GMC, he knew his team still had two tough conference games on their schedule, and neither he nor his team could afford to start celebrating yet. A loss to either one of their next two opponents—the Middle Georgia College Wolverines, who they defeated in their first game of the season, or the Gordon College Cadets, who had a history of being a difficult conference rival—would eliminate them from the title race.

Beyond that, Bowden felt that the outcome of these next two games would decide for him personally whether his first year as a head coach was successful or not.

South Georgia had defeated Middle Georgia College in their season-opening game, but Bowden was smart enough to know that beating the same team twice in the same year would be difficult. However, he was comforted knowing that his team would have the home-field advantage and a homecoming crowd full of South Georgia alumni to cheer them on.

As expected, when the Tigers lined up against the Wolverines on November 12 for their second meeting of the 1955 season, the stands were packed with a boisterous crowd of South Georgia supporters.

South Georgia fans grew even more exuberant when the Tigers kicked off to the Wolverines and forced them to punt the football from their 25-yard line after their first series of downs.

Ronnie Kelley brought the packed house to its feet when he returned the punt almost 35 yards to the Wolverines' 18-yard line.

On the next two plays, Kelley and Blinkey Barber banged out enough yardage to move the ball to the 7-yard line. Then, on the Tigers' third offensive play of the game, Kelley raced across the goal line, scoring the game's first touchdown. Homer Sowell added the point-after-touchdown, and while the game was still early in the first quarter, the Tigers went ahead of the Wolverines by 7 points.

The game's pace slowed considerably after the touchdown, even though the Tigers kept threatening to add points to their lead.

Early in the second quarter, things picked up when Roger Wilkinson and Homer Sowell combined their efforts and upped the Tigers lead to 14 points. The score stayed the same for the remainder of the half, but it was clear that the contest was one-sided in favor of the Tigers.

Statistically, the Tigers picked up 10 first downs, rushed for 131 yards, and passed for 64 yards, compared to Middle Georgia's 1 first down, 3 yards rushing, and 30 yards passing. When the second half started, the Tigers continued to dominate the game, scoring three more touchdowns.

Blinkey Barber got credit for scoring the first TD when he dove into the end zone from 1 yard out after the Tigers put together a successful 88-yard drive.

Their second touchdown was the result of a razzle-dazzle double reverse that Wilkinson started when he handed the football off to Ronnie Kelley. Kelley, who was running to his right behind a protective wall of Tiger linemen, flipped the ball backward to Gene "Doodlebug" Edwards who was running in the opposite direction toward the left side of the field. After Edwards snatched Kelley's lateral, he circled around the left side of the Tigers' line and dashed 26 yards to the Wolverines' 12-yard line. On the next play, Kelley brought the drive to its finality when he raced into pay dirt, scoring their fourth touchdown.

The Tigers scored their final touchdown when the Wolverines' quarterback attempted to throw a quick look-in pass over the middle of the line. Roger Wilkinson, who was playing linebacker on defense, stepped in front of their intended receiver, grabbed the football, and high-stepped it back across the Wolverines' goal line.

With a 27-point lead in the third quarter, Bowden tried to give as many reserve players as he could some valuable game experience. Unfortunately, the substitutions also gave the Wolverines a chance to come back and score two touchdowns, reducing the Tigers' lead to 15 points.

With the score standing at 33-18, Bowden rallied his starting team back onto the field and closed the door on the Wolverines' threat for the rest of the game.

The Tigers' second victory of the season over Middle Georgia College gave them a conference record of four wins and no defeats, and made it possible for them to play the Gordon Military College Cadets for the coveted championship trophy in their final game of the season.

South Georgia Tigers vs Gordon Military Bulldog Cadets

SINCE GORDON WAS ALSO UNDEFEATED in conference play, the Tigers' victory celebration after defeating Middle Georgia was abbreviated if not non-existent. After coming this far through a very topsy-turvy year, Bowden wasn't about to let his players get too excited or relaxed while the championship was still at stake.

Some players remember the practices from the week leading up to the championship game as some of the roughest they had had since the first two weeks of the season when they were practicing twice a day. "We ran so much that week that we stomped the living crap out of the last few sprigs of crabgrass on our playing field," said Ape Adams, a linemen.

The last week of practice brought some unexpected bad news to the Tigers when Bowden found out that two of the team's leading ground gainers, Bobby Dixon and Everett Graham, wouldn't be able to play in the final game because of injuries. The team would have to depend on Blinkey Barber and Doodlebug Edwards to fill in and pick up any slack left by Dixon and Graham's absence.

No one questioned Barber's ability because he had already played in almost every game and had proven he was more than capable of carrying his share of the load. Edwards, on the other hand, didn't have the game experience that Barber had, but he was one of the team's fastest players, so Bowden was optimistic that he would be able to handle the job once he got over the initial jitters of starting his first game.

The Tigers arrived in Barnesville, Georgia, on November 19, and the game against the Gordon Bulldog Cadets got underway as scheduled that evening.

The first quarter was a slow defensive grind. It appeared that both teams were more concerned with defending their goal line and avoiding any costly errors than they were in mounting an aggressive offensive attack and testing their opponent.

By the second quarter, the Tigers relaxed and played more aggressively on offense and the game slowly began to change in their favor. They were able to get closer and closer to Gordon's end zone every time they had possession of the football. Twice they even got inside Gordon's 15-yard line and appeared unstoppable, but both times they managed to stop themselves by committing some mental error.

Finally, during the latter part of the second quarter, after they stopped killing themselves on every drive with their own mistakes, the Tigers scored the game's first touchdown.

Ronnie Kelley was credited with the score after he faked inside a charging Cadet defender, spun away, and raced across the goal line. Because Kelley and the Gordon player he escaped from had played together on the same high school team, Kelley couldn't help but taunt him a little after scoring the game's first TD—telling him to pick up his jockey in the Tigers' locker room after the game. That was just about as trashy as trash talk got in the 1950s.

After that, South Georgia was able to hang onto their 6-point lead until the first half ended.

When the second half got underway and the Cadets received the kickoff, they immediately put together their best offensive show of the night. After returning the kickoff to their 47-yard line, the Cadets needed only three plays to get across the Tigers' goal line, tie the score, and break the deadlock by successfully converting the PAT.

The 7–6 score held until late in the third quarter when the Tigers forced a Cadet fumble and Ape Adams jumped on the ball at the Cadets' 28-yard line. The turnover shifted the game's momentum back to the Tigers, and it wasn't long before Kelley scampered into pay dirt, scoring their second touchdown.

That second touchdown eventually gave the Tigers a 12-7 victory and the conference championship.

Although the score didn't reflect it, the Tigers consistently out-played the Cadets in the fourth quarter. If the Tigers hadn't impeded themselves with penalties, there would have been two more touch-downs on the scoreboard. But Coach Bowden didn't have any problem praising his entire team after the game, stating that he was especially proud of their linemen who he described as "the strength of our team all year." He also said, "They seemed to get better and more cohesive with every game."

In particular he singled out: Bull Smith, a military veteran with the physique and stamina that any Mr. Universe would envy; Richard Johnson, who could probably play on any major college football team; Monty Roberts, who played every play as if he believed the outcome of every game depended solely on him; Homer Sowell, a steady and reliable military veteran who played three years of service football in Alaska before coming to South Georgia; Cecil Morris, who willingly sacrificed himself on almost every play for the good of the team; Rosby Mulkey, another military veteran whose quiet, tough, and steadfast demeanor earned him the respect of his team-mates as well as his adversaries; Charles Gulbrandsen, who survived combat in Korea as an army grunt, and who played and led with the quiet, strong convictions of an individual who appreciated the opportunity just to compete; Bobby Keys, one of the team's captains, whose steady, hard-working take-no-prisoners attitude earned him the admiration of both his coaches and teammates; Ape Adams, who never met a person he didn't like—or an opponent on a football field he didn't like to hit; Stumpy Franklin, who hit opponents like a cannonball on every play and believed his assignment was always to keep hitting until there weren't any opponents left standing; Reverend Cooper, whose intelligence, work ethic, and fortitude allowed him to play in the trenches and succeed against much larger linemen; and Jerry Holland, whose dependability and tough mental focus made him the centerpiece of one of the best junior college lines in the country.

The South Georgia team that captured the Georgia State Junior College Conference Championship in 1955 was made up of twenty-eight freshmen and eight sophomores.

Ronnie Kelley was their top point-getter for the season, scoring a total of 48 points. He was followed by Roger Wilkinson with 36, Everett Graham with 25, Homer Sowell with 16, Bobby Dixon with 12, Blinkey Barber with 7, and Richard Johnson and Billy Thornton with 6 each.

At the conclusion of the season, Bobby Keys and Ronnie Kelley were officially selected as members of the Williamson Junior College All-American team. Keys was selected as a member of the top thirty-three-man squad, and Kelley was chosen as an honorable mention member. They were the only two players from the state of Georgia selected for the "dream team." It was also the first time in the history of South Georgia football that two players from the same team had received this special recognition.

When Bowden had a chance to look back at the season and reflect on everything that had happened, he commended all of his players for the way they worked together to make the season and his first year as their head football coach a success. He has said many times since that he was especially proud of the way they recovered from three crushing losses in the early part of the season to win the conference title.

08

WELL, I LOVE YOU
MORE THAN I DO BASKETBALL

fter South Georgia's football team won the 1955
Georgia State Junior College Championship and Bowden
completed his first season as their head coach, a completely different
challenge awaited him: basketball—a sport he was convinced he wasn't
qualified to coach and a challenge he wasn't looking forward to. He
had limited time to prepare for the basketball season, which increased
his uneasiness considerably.

Today, a new coach like Bowden, who was just taking over the
head-coaching duties of a sport, would have several months to get
ready and at least a couple of assistants to help out. Bowden however,
didn't have that luxury at South Georgia. In fact, he didn't even have
one assistant, and he only had a very few short weeks to prepare
himself and his team before the season started.

To complicate his situation even more, most of his preparation
had to be done during the Christmas holidays—a time when he
desperately needed to find a second job to supplement his small
coaching salary. With money and basketball weighing heavily on
his mind, he didn't have a lot of extra time to relax and spend with
his family, but the lack of time did force him to figure out some
priorities pretty quickly.

With three small children at home anxiously waiting Santa
Claus's arrival on December 25, he quickly established finding a
job and earning some extra money as his highest priority. Once this
was decided, it didn't take him long to get a job at the post office
delivering mail during the Christmas holidays.

The post office job became an annual ritual for Bowden during his tenure at South Georgia.

When he took the job, he thought he would be able to deliver mail and still have enough time to prepare himself for the approaching basketball season. But the truth was, he wouldn't have been able to adequately prepare for the basketball season even if he had done nothing but study throughout the entire holiday.

His complete lack of success on the basketball court left his critics plenty of room to question his ability to coach basketball. Like the old cliché says, man cannot serve two masters.

To be completely fair to Bowden, the situation and the difficulties he faced were unbelievable and would never be accepted today. There hasn't been a coaching job in America for more than half a century, or maybe even longer, that would require any one person to go through what he went through in 1955 and 1956.

To begin with, he was the head coach of the school's football, basketball, and baseball teams, as well as the athletic director. During football season he had one assistant, but during basketball and baseball season he was completely on his own. Not only did he not have an assistant coach during the basketball and baseball seasons, he didn't have any other paid staff to help him with any of his responsibilities—no athletic trainer, equipment manager, or secretary.

Because he had no assistance of any kind, Bowden had to take care of every task imaginable just to keep his teams together and on the playing fields, or court depending on the season, in addition to coaching.

Any one of these head-coaching positions or his position as athletic director would be considered a full-time job today. And no one in his right mind would even consider accepting the responsibilities of any of these jobs without the help of a full staff.

Even for a coach with years of experience, it would be a very difficult undertaking. For Bowden, being new and inexperienced, it was enormous. Consider that he had no one to train him or point him in the right direction and it becomes mind-boggling.

In today's coaching community, a similar situation would require at least two or three head coaches and a half dozen or more assistants, plus several secretaries, trainers, equipment managers, and more.

His coaching responsibilities were lumped on top of the stresses of being a young husband and father with a family growing by leaps and bounds. Occasionally he even had to pick up a second or even a third job just to pay the bills.

Considering the situation, it's no wonder basketball didn't go well.

Amazingly, some critics still believed that the reason he wasn't successful as a basketball coach was because he didn't like basketball or that he didn't try hard enough, but to anyone who knows Bowden, that's ludicrous. (And that's expressing it gentlemanly.) Bowden never disputed the fact that he didn't want to coach basketball, but the notion that he didn't try hard enough is ridiculous, especially once you understand his competitive spirit and his dedication to responsibility. To state it simply, it didn't matter if Bowden was coaching, or playing, football or basketball or baseball or golf or horseshoes or Ping-Pong or anything else, he always gave his all.

But for the sake of argument, let's concede that he and basketball were not a good match. Add to that the fact that in the Georgia State Junior College Conference there were at least twelve schools in which basketball was the main athletic program—and some of them were pretty good.

Probably the best and most prominent team in the conference was Brewton-Parker. Brewton-Parker was a very small school in Mount Vernon, Georgia, and almost every year their basketball team won the conference title. Because of their reputation and consistent winning record, they usually played in several post-season national tournaments.

The first time South Georgia played Brewton-Parker under Bowden's leadership, they played on Brewton-Parker's home court and the final score was so one-sided that none of the South Georgia players will admit that they can remember it.

Later, around mid-season, they were scheduled to play again.

This time South Georgia would be on their home court, and they were determined that their second meeting would not be a repeat of their first. Bowden had schooled his players to believe that even if they were not as skilled as the Brewton-Parker players, they could still out-hustle them, and if they out-hustled them, it would make a big difference in the final score and the game's outcome.

With their second contest underway, it appeared that the Tigers' hustle was working just as Bowden had suggested. The South Georgia players were clearly out-hustling the Brewton-Parker players, and as a result they were matching their opponent's score point for point. The South Georgia College gymnasium was packed with an overly enthusiastic student body hoping for a major upset.

As the game progressed, Bowden began to sense that something was amiss and that the Brewton-Parker team on the court couldn't possibly be the same team they had played earlier in the season. Indeed, a few minutes later he discovered that their first team was actually sitting in the stands watching the game and had not even put on their uniforms.

That hit Bowden, and his players, like a ton of bricks. Bowden had never pretended to care a lot about basketball, but he still had his pride and competitive spirit. Not only was Brewton-Parker's ruse a bold face put-down, Bowden took it as a personal affront to him and his players. The Tigers were so infuriated they played even more aggressively and with a newfound determination, and by the end of the first half, they were actually leading by a small margin.

Their zeal, although natural and reasonable, backfired on South Georgia once the second half got underway. Their success in the first half left the Brewton-Parker coach no choice but to get his first team out of the stands and onto the court to play the second half. This changed things completely, and it didn't matter how much determination the Tigers played with or how much they hustled; they were still no match for Brewton-Parker's first team.

Brewton-Parker quickly rearranged the numbers on the scoreboard, and the Tigers' nightmarish first game came back to haunt them.

Minutes seemed like hours, and the longer the game lasted, the more life Brewton-Parker squeezed out of the once-unshakable Tigers. When the game finally ended, Brewton-Parker had more than doubled their score and was leading the Tigers by at least 40 points.

Bud Holt, who led the Tigers in scoring that night, recalls that he was so embarrassed during the second half that all he wanted to do was get off the court. "I just wanted to get off the court and hide somewhere," he said. "Mudville" was nothing compared to the torment Bowden and his basketball team suffered that night.

The rest of the season only brought more woe. In one game, the Tigers' opponent started a full-court press almost immediately after the opening tip-off. The defense gave the Tigers so much trouble that they could hardly get the ball past the midcourt line. Bowden was so frustrated at one point during the game, he let his football coaching skills overpower his basketball knowledge—or to be more accurate, his lack of knowledge.

He called Ronnie Kelley, who was a guard on the basketball team but a running back on the Tigers' football team, to the side of the court and told him that the next time he was pressed and couldn't dribble the ball down court, he should tuck the ball under his arm, lower his head, and just plow straight ahead. Bowden apparently thought that since this worked in football, it should also work in basketball.

By the end of the season, Bowden's incompatibility with basketball was obvious. He has admitted that his basketball coaching experience was "awful" and often "embarrassing," which is pretty well illustrated by the team's final record of eighteen losses and one win.

The only team they were able to defeat was a pick-up team of sailors from Glynco Naval Air Station, a small navy base in Brunswick, Georgia. After that game, Bowden was quoted as saying, "The only reason we won that game was because the Navy team was worse than our team, not because we were better."

In many ways, Bowden's difficulties in basketball worried him more than his problems in football because he was concerned about the effect that losing was having on his players, especially as individuals—much more than how it was affecting him personally.

One of his worst memories from his basketball experience happened midway through the season. One of his players got so discouraged that he quit the team and decided he would never play basketball again.

John Albert Williams, a high school all-state player from Montezuma, Georgia, whose high school basketball team won the state championship his senior year, came to South Georgia and played basketball for Bowden his freshman year. He was by far the best player on the team, and when he quit, the loss was huge. That wasn't what Bowden was concerned about though. More than anything else, Bowden felt responsible for the emotional pain that caused him to quit. He was also worried that quitting would have an impact on John later in life. Considering all of this, he exercised his authority as athletic director after the season was over and fired himself as the Tigers' basketball coach.

DURING HIS FIRST YEAR AT SOUTH GEORGIA, Bowden was so busy taking care of all his different coaching duties and athletic director's responsibilities, as well as working extra jobs to keep his head above water financially, he rarely had any time to spend with his family. Even when he did have a little time, according to his wife, Ann, he couldn't stop talking about football or something related to football.

Ann, whose day at home with three small children was every bit as stressful as her husband's, wanted to talk about something other than football on one of the rare evenings that Bobby was home. She tried to change the subject several times while Bobby was talking, but every time she thought she'd succeeded, he managed to steer the conversation back to football.

Finally, Ann got so fed up that she snapped. "Bobby, sometimes I believe that you love football more than you do me."

Bowden knew she was upset, so he waited a moment before saying anything. When he did respond, he said in a very sheepish and subdued voice, "Well, I love you more than I do basketball."

09

COLLEGE LIFE BETWEEN
FOOTBALL SEASONS

Pranks

In the off-season, South Georgia football players had plenty of idle time to relax and get involved in the more leisurely side of college life. A few of the players decided their down time should be used in creative ways—like getting involved in a prank or antic. Looking back on those years, one particularly creative prank and one specific player always come to mind.

Billy Franklin, who everyone called Stumpy or Ole Stumpy, was only about 5' 6" tall, but he weighed about 195 pounds. Bowden has often said, "Stumpy was the toughest son of a gun, pound for pound, I ever coached." He was ornery as heck and, more often than not, the instigator of some prank. One of the most memorable pranks, however, turned the table on Stumpy and he learned what it was like to be the victim.

This infamous prank began one afternoon during an innocent Ping-Pong game. Bull Smith and Blinkey Barber were playing a game, and Stumpy and Ape Adams were watching them impatiently.

This Ping-Pong room was just big enough for one ping-pong table and a few folding chairs.

Stumpy and Ape, who were always arguing about something, were bickering as usual. After a few minutes, Stumpy told Ape he was through arguing with him, and he stood up and asked Bull and Blinkey if he could play the next game.

Not to be slighted, Ape jumped up and announced, "I was here first, so I'm going to play next." He eyed Stumpy and told him, "You might as well sit back down until it's your turn."

Now, everybody, including Stumpy, knew that Ape had never played Ping-Pong before and had only said he wanted to play to antagonize Stumpy.

Stumpy and Ape started fighting all over again until Stumpy decided to plead his case and ask Bull and Blinkey who they thought should play the next game. When Bull said that he thought it should be Ape and Blinkey agreed, Stumpy went bonkers and accused Bull and Blinkey of purposely dragging out their game just to keep him from playing and ganging up against him with Ape.

But Bull and Blinkey weren't listening. Not only had they turned a deaf ear to Stumpy's ranting, they'd also started their game over, but this time, they played even slower.

Stumpy was livid, turning red in the face and complaining louder than ever.

After letting Stumpy bellow for a few minutes, Ape yelled, "Stumpy, you jackass, look what you've done. You've made Bull and Blinkey mad. Now neither of us will to get to play." He sat down, calmly folded his arms across his chest, stretched his feet out in front of him, and told Stumpy, "You might as well sit down too."

Stumpy, however, went right on bellyaching until not even Ape was listening to him. When it dawned on him that no one was paying attention to him anymore, he stopped shouting and stood quietly, hands on his hips, glaring at the Ping-Pong table.

For a few moments the only sound in the room was Stumpy's heavy breathing and the steady patter of the Ping-Pong ball hitting paddle or table. In the quiet, Stumpy suddenly reached across the table, snatched the ball, dropped it to the floor, and stomped it flat.

Shocked, Ape, Bull, and Blinkey stood in dead silence while Stumpy ran out of the building, grumbling over his shoulder as he left.

Since the ball that Stumpy demolished was the only one in the student center, Ping-Pong came to a screeching halt, and Ape, Bull, and Blinkey were left with nothing to do but stew.

Back in the dorm, they told Milton Cooper what had happened, and together they plotted a way to even the score with Stumpy.

So began one of the biggest pranks of the year at South Georgia College.

Stumpy was going to regret the errors of his ways for a very long time if they had anything to do with it. The first thing they needed was a fish—or in Bull's words, "a big ole mullet." It seemed that this group believed that Bull was some sort of an expert on fish and fish smells, so when he said that an "ole mullet" would work better than any other fish, they all agreed.

After Cooper volunteered to pay for the fish, they started finalizing their plot and assigning tasks.

The next morning Bull, Ape, and Cooper went to a fish market in Douglas and bought the biggest "ole mullet" Cooper could afford. Later that same day, Blinkey talked Stumpy into going to town with him to shoot some pool at a local pool hall.

It was necessary to get Stumpy away from campus long enough for Bull, Ape, and Cooper to get into his room, slit his mattress open along a seam on the underside, stuff the mullet inside, sew the mattress back together, and get out of the room.

Once they were finished, all they'd have to do was wait a few hours before the fun began.

By the next day, the pungent odor of the rotting fish filled Stumpy's room. Because he couldn't figure out what the smell was, he asked anyone he could find in the dorm to come to his room and see if they could figure out what was causing the "terrible odor." But by then, just about everyone in the building knew what was going on, so their standard reply was always "What odor?" or "What smell?"

A couple days later, the stench was so bad around Stumpy's room that no one wanted to go near it—including Stumpy and his roommate, Roger Wilkinson, who knew about the prank, but had been sworn to secrecy. It had gotten so bad, in fact, that Stumpy and Wilkinson were already camping out in a vacant room at the opposite end of the hallway.

With every passing day, the smell got a little worse and Stumpy got a little more frustrated. Finally, he decided, after around-the-room sniffing, that the source of the smell had to be his mattress, but since he couldn't figure out why, he took the mattress and traded it for another one that he found in an unoccupied room.

Stumpy might have solved his problem if he'd kept the switch a secret—and his room had had time to air out. But since he told everyone he could what he had done, as soon as he left the building, Ape and Bull moved the stinking mattress right back into his room.

When Stumpy returned to the dorm and found his room still reeking of the same repulsive odor, he went ballistic, cussing everything in sight. At one point, his roommate even found him walking in circles, mumbling to himself about what he was going to do when he found out who had done this to his room.

Finally, at the absolute end of his rope, Stumpy heaved the mattress out a second-floor dorm window. The mattress lay crushed and abandoned in front of the building—until a faculty member saw it and an investigation was initiated by the school's administration.

The investigation created so much talk and gossip among the students and cast so much attention on Stumpy that the dean of students personally invited Stumpy to his office for a private talk. During their discussion, Stumpy made a full confession, was admonished, and lost his room deposit—something he's still trying to get reimbursed for to this day.

About eighteen months after the incident, when Stumpy left South Georgia for a tour of duty with the U.S. Army, he was still in the dark as to what had actually happened. Almost forty-five years passed before Ape and Bull finally told him the truth. "It's kind of funny now," Stumpy said, "but it sure wasn't funny at the time." But he added a warning to all those involved saying, "This ain't over! This Stump ain't dead yet!"

Spring Training

IN 1956, SPRING TRAINING STARTED in the middle of February. Players either loved or hated spring training. Those that loved it wanted the opportunity to show the coaches they deserved a place on the team, or maybe even the first team. Those that hated it, hated it because all they had to look forward to were long, exhausting practices, where they ate a lot of dust and dirt.

Bowden's outlook, especially between the 1955 and 1956 seasons, was a little more positive. Spring training meant he could get back to his real love: coaching football. It was also his first spring training since taking the job at South Georgia, and he was eager to get started.

On the first day of practice, he and Coach Mrvos issued uniforms to approximately thirty-five aspiring players, including several who were returning from the previous year's team.

Any uncertainties or anxieties Bowden had during his first football season were now behind him. Spring training was going to give him advantages he didn't have his first year, such as the opportunity to experiment with different ideas and formations before deciding which ones he wanted to utilize during the regular season.

Even though he expected a much larger number of players when the regular season actually started in September, spring training was also going to give him a chance to evaluate the progress of several returning players, as well as look at some new players.

He and Mrvos both believed that one of the biggest difficulties they would face in 1956 would be replacing three key players who would graduate at the end of the school year. Those three players were Bobby Keys, Ronnie Kelley, and Monty Roberts. All three were considered team leaders in 1955 and were responsible for much of the team's success. Bowden and Mrvos both expected several of the returning lettermen to step forward in spring training and fill those vacated leadership positions.

According to *The Douglas Enterprise*, a local newspaper, several new candidates were vying for a place on the Tigers' 1956 team. Those candidates included: Charles Perry, a tackle from Douglas, Georgia; Jimmy Bowen, a running back from Waycross, Georgia; Sonny Letson, a guard from Atlanta, Georgia; and Larry DeLoach, another running back from Glennville, Georgia. The article reported that "DeLoach and Bowen are expected to add a lot of speed to the backfield."

After Coach Bowden announced his expectations and established some rules that he expected the players to comply with, spring training started at a rugged pace with contact drills beginning on the second day. Several returning lettermen—including running backs Graham and Barber, and quarterbacks Wilkinson and Studdard—seemed eager to step forward and fill the leadership roles left by Keys, Kelley, and Roberts.

The work ethic of the lettermen set a good example for the new players, and together they started developing what seemed like a winning nucleus for the coming year.

According to Bowden, spring training was expected to last four weeks and would conclude on March 10 with an inter-squad game-type scrimmage. Because Bowden still had a strong desire to start some type of recruiting program, he wrote letters to a number of high schools throughout the state to announce that South Georgia would hold tryouts from March 7–10, and that graduating high school football players interested in playing for the Tigers in 1956 should try out.

At first, his letter didn't generate the response Bowden had hoped for, but later, when the season got closer, it did inspire several recently graduated high school players, as well as a few players who were already playing at other colleges or universities to consider South Georgia.

Bowden considered spring training to have been a success, primarily because he and Mrvos accomplished most of their objectives, including distinguishing new players they believed would help the team in its new season. They also had a chance to look at areas they believed needed strengthening, and to experiment with some new ideas they were thinking of incorporating into their plans for the 1956 team.

All the players who attended spring training were excited about their team's future, and they started looking forward to the next football season.

Lazy Days of Spring

AFTER SPRING TRAINING, most football players returned their attention to campus—or, more accurately, returned their attention to bringing a little spice to South Georgia's campus.

One too calm spring day, Tiger teammates Ape, Blinkey, Bull, and Vernon Brinson went to the local barber and requested Mohawks. Now, the Mohawk was not a pervasive hairstyle in the 1950s. This was the era of blue jeans and poodle skirts, ponytails and crew cuts; seeing a Mohawk was not an everyday occurrence, which is probably why the grooming appeared in the local newspaper.

Although the Mohawk didn't catch on with the rest of the football team, it did eventually lead to another interesting style. Stumpy, of mattress-hurling fame, was not willing to be outdone by four guys with Mohawks. So when fall practice began in September 1956, he created his own coiffure by completely shaving his head except for a large V in the middle of his head. Stumpy's head was probably the only head large and flat enough to accommodate the V, so he alone sported the victory symbol during football season.

Besides spontaneous haircuts, several football players turned their attention back to mischief after the long, brutal spring training session. This time, instead of outwitting each other, they targeted those they wanted to impress: girls.

All in the name of good fun, two, or maybe three, football players, whose identity won't be revealed for their own protection (or because the statute of limitations for their heinous crime might not have expired), conned an "innocent coed" into being an accomplice in one of their pranks.

The perpetrators prepared for the prank much the way they had for a previous panty raid, for which a mole inside the girls' dorm was needed. This prank, however, was different in some respects, and it was later dubbed the "Boom Boom Caper."

After successfully recruiting their accomplice, the Caper Cohorts went to work plotting to create some excitement in the girls' dormitory.

In 1956, campus rules required all female students living in the dorm to be in their rooms by 9:30 p.m. on weeknights and by 11 p.m. on Friday and Saturday nights. Male students were only allowed in the dorm's lounge area but never after these hours. Ma Bowman (Ms. Charles Bowman), the dormitory housemother, was always present to enforce the rules.

Once the lounge clock struck the curfew hour, all doors and windows were shut, locked, and secured by a designated student proctor.

At the appointed hour, the cohorts' accomplice had to open the window at the north end of the second-floor hallway of the girls' dorm. The open window would allow the pranksters to throw cherry bombs into the hallway.

Because the cohorts had perfected their plan down to the last detail, it was executed with military precision. And when the firecrackers exploded inside the dormitory, screams poured out of the building for what seemed like several minutes.

Immediately after the explosions, Ma Bowman and several other school officials ran frantically through the building trying to determine what had caused the loud booming noise. Later, after the dorm had finally calmed down, they decided that it was just another mischievous prank.

Even after the initial excitement died down, the event continued to be the topic of discussion at late-night gab sessions where coeds entertained themselves by speculating who they thought the culprits were.

Swimming Pool Area

LATER THAT SPRING, as the temperature climbed, the outdoor swimming pool behind the gymnasium opened. Once open, it quickly became a gathering place for a large number of the student body, including most of the football team, who spent as much time as they could in the pool area. Faculty members, including Bowden, and their families were also regular visitors.

The relaxed atmosphere at the pool gave the students and faculty an opportunity to get to know each other in a less restricted environment. It was an atmosphere the football players enjoyed, but it was often difficult for Bowden, who initially felt he needed to maintain a certain amount of distance from his players in order to be effective as their coach. It was especially difficult when one of his players challenged him to participate in what they generally referred to as a "friendly game" of horseshoes. More often than not, when this happened, he'd drop his guarded aloofness and accept the challenge.

One afternoon after he accepted one of their challenges, the game got very intense almost immediately, which was typical anytime Bowden was involved in any type of competition.

While the game was being played, Bowden's youngest son, Tommy, who was still in diapers and not completely steady on his feet, was wandering around picking up pine cones and investigating nature as kids his age are inclined to do.

When it was Bowden's turn to pitch, he picked up three shoes, stepped to the pitching line, and focused on his toss. Being the competitor that he was and still is today, he was completely oblivious to everything else around him.

By the time he was ready to throw his third and final shoe, nothing short of an exploding bomb could have broken his concentration. As Bowden stepped into his pitch, hand swinging back, little Tommy ran up behind him. In mid-toss, the horseshoe in Bowden's hand collided with Tommy's head, knocking him to the ground.

Several students watching the game gasped and ran toward Tommy. Bowden, however, who was still focusing on his game, seemed completely unaware that he'd hit anything. Even after completing his pitch, he never looked back before walking out to the pitching box to add up his score.

Tommy, equally oblivious, wobbled to his feet and tried to walk off in the opposite direction. When the student observers tried to examine him, they realized he was more annoyed by their attention than hurt, so they released him and he rambled away from the game area.

The game continued without Bowden being told anything about the accident.

10

SUMMER BREAK WASN'T
A BREAK EITHER

Hiring an Assistant

*A*t the end of the spring quarter, after all of SGC's athletic programs had finished for the school year, Bowden had a little time to get some things accomplished before he had to start thinking seriously about the 1956 football season.

First he had to find a replacement for his only assistant football coach, Sam Mrvos, who resigned to accept a job at the University of Georgia. Bowden knew almost immediately that he wanted Vince Gibson, an old high school and college friend and teammate, to fill that position. Gibson had just graduated from Florida State University and accepted a high school assistant coaching position in St. Augustine, Florida. But that didn't stop Bowden from calling him and offering him the position at South Georgia. When Gibson seemed a little reluctant about moving to South Georgia, Bowden kept prodding until Gibson finally agreed to think about the offer and let him know his decision in a couple of days.

As soon as he agreed to think about it, Bowden knew he was persuadable, so he told Gibson he would drive to St. Augustine the next day so they could discuss the opportunities he would have at South Georgia in more detail.

Just as Bowden promised, he loaded his family into their car the next day and took off for St. Augustine.

When they left South Georgia, neither he nor his wife had any cash on them, but Bowden had a Gulf credit card that he could use at any Gulf station to buy any gas or snacks they would need, so he assumed they wouldn't need any cash. He mapped out an easy 300-mile round trip through Jacksonville and over the St. Johns River. What he hadn't planned on, though, was the cost of the toll to cross the river.

When they got to the St. Johns River, the tollbooth operator informed Bowden the toll was 35 cents and that he couldn't accept a Gulf credit card. Bowden was forced to turn around, drive back through Jacksonville, and take a longer route to St. Augustine. The detour added about seventy-five more miles and three more hours to their round trip, and it made the trip a lot more difficult than Bowden had initially anticipated.

However frustrated he was, it didn't affect his sales pitch, because after they talked, Gibson agreed to come to South Georgia, even though he knew he would be making less money than he had been promised in St. Augustine.

A few weeks later, after Gibson and his new wife moved to Douglas, Bowden informed him that, in addition to being his assistant football coach, he was also going to be the head basketball coach and teach girls' physical education. But he assured Gibson that being a head coach in any sport would look good on his resume.

In 1957, Bowden also assigned Gibson the head coaching responsibilities of the track team after the Georgia State Junior College Conference decided to start an intercollegiate track program.

Whether Bowden was candid with Gibson about basketball and teaching phys ed when he convinced him to come to South Georgia, no one but Bowden knows for sure, but Gibson accepted the additional duties with enthusiasm. Like any young coach, he hoped to improve his chances of some day moving up the coaching ranks.

With enthusiasm and a lot of hard work, Gibson successfully turned South Georgia's basketball program around and built a successful track program during the next three years.

Later, at the end of the 1958 school year, after he had gained experience as an assistant football coach and had been the head coach of two successful programs, Gibson left South Georgia for a major university. First, he went to work as an assistant football coach at Florida State University and then at the University of Tennessee, but it didn't take him long to snare the head coach position at Kansas State University where he stayed for eight years and built a very successful football program. Later, he led the football programs at both the University of Louisville and Tulane University.

Finding a Part-time Job

AFTER HIRING GIBSON to be his assistant, Bowden started looking for a summer job that would help him defray the ever-increasing financial needs of his growing family, which now included him, his wife, and their four children: Robyn, Steve, Tommy, and Terry.

He found work at a large tobacco warehouse in Douglas where his primary responsible was to unload, weigh, and stack tobacco bales brought to the warehouse by area farmers. He worked from 8 p.m. to 8 a.m. seven nights a week. Even by 1950s' standards, this was hard labor, but since he was making almost a dollar an hour, it was also consider good summer employment.

Bowden says he was pretty busy during the early hours of the night, but around two or three in the morning when things slowed down, he could usually count on getting a couple hours sleep before he got off the next morning. When he did have a chance to get some sleep, he made sure to be on the highest stack of bales he could find. He made the mistake of napping on the floor one night, and he learned that the warehouse rats not only weren't afraid of him, but considered him a good meal.

Recruiting

EVEN THOUGH HE WAS WORKING seven nights a week, Bowden still hadn't given up his dream of starting a recruiting program. And, if possible, he wanted to recruit a couple of players before the season started.

Unfortunately, he had to put the dream aside before he even got started because he got another summer job as a lifeguard. Having another job had to come before recruiting.

As a lifeguard, he would work from 9 a.m. to 5 p.m. seven days a week, which he didn't expect to interfere with his night job at the warehouse, but it sure didn't leave him a lot of time to do anything else, including recruiting.

There was one exception, however, and that exception was Bobby Pate, from Fitzgerald, Georgia. Pate had just graduated from high school and for some reason had been overlooked by most of the major colleges in the area. Shortly after Pate's graduation, a businessman from Fitzgerald contacted Bowden and asked him to consider Pate for a scholarship to play football at South Georgia. Pate had worked summers for the man, and he believed Pate deserved a chance to play football at the college level. Being an alumnus of South Georgia, he felt it was a good match for Pate.

SINCE BOWDEN WAS WORKING DAY AND NIGHT, he arranged for Pate to meet him at the tobacco warehouse one night. When they finally got together, Pate brought along a scrapbook his mother had kept that highlighted his accomplishments as a high school football player and member of the track team. After reviewing Pate's scrapbook and talking with him, Bowden was happy to encourage him to come to South Georgia, but he couldn't offer him any financial assistance because there wasn't any money left in their scholarship fund.

Once Bowden discussed the scholarship shortfall with Pate's former employer, the gentleman agreed to donate the cost of Pate's tuition as well as the cost of his room and board to South Georgia's scholarship fund. Pate therefore attended South Georgia on a full football scholarship, and became Bowden's first officially recruited football player.

Bowden recruited Pate the same way he accepted the job at South Georgia—on blind faith but with a gut feeling that it was the right thing to do. As it turned out, his gut feeling paid off for both of them. Pate became one of the most successful players and coaches he has ever recruited.

In 1956, Pate broke into the Tigers' starting lineup around midseason as a freshman running back. From that point forward, he started almost every game, making the Georgia State Junior College Conference All-State First Team in 1957.

Once he completed two years at South Georgia, Pate accepted a full football scholarship to play at Presbyterian College in Clinton, South Carolina. In his senior year at Presbyterian College, he led his team through a 9-1 season, a national ranking in small-college football, and an invitation to play in the Tangerine Bowl. All three were firsts for Presbyterian College.

In that same year, he was selected as a first team member of the Williamson Little All-America team and named South Carolina's "Back of the Year" in college football. When he graduated from Presbyterian, he was drafted by the San Francisco 49ers, but instead of playing professional football, he chose to follow in Bowden's footsteps and go into coaching.

After several very successful years as a head coach at the high-school level, he accepted a position as an assistant to Coach Bobby Waters at Western Carolina University in North Carolina. He stayed at Western Carolina until he was offered the head coach position at the University of West Georgia in Carrolton, Georgia, in 1980.

When he accepted the job at West Georgia, the university was entering Division III, and Pate was hired to organize and initiate their program. During Pate's first two years at West Georgia, his teams won twenty-one games and lost one. His second year, they won the Division III national championship, and Pate was named "Coach of the Year" in Division III. In 1985, when West Georgia moved up into a Division II conference, Pate decided to resign and return to his first love: coaching at the high-school level. He started and finished his thirty-year coaching career in Hart County, Georgia.

In 1989, Pate was inducted into the University of West Georgia's Athletic Hall of Fame.

Reminiscing

AT A SOUTH GEORGIA REUNION not long after Pate was recognized for his success as a football player and coach, Larry DeLoach, a Tiger from the 1956 football team, teased Bowden about Pate's starting role. He apologized to him for doubting that he would ever be a successful football coach, explaining that for a long time he'd questioned Bowden's ability to choose the best players because he'd chosen Pate to start ahead of him. DeLoach broke into a smile and got a big laugh from Bowden and all of his former teammates.

This was typical of the joking and laughing that takes place at South Georgia Tiger reunions and an example of the camaraderie the players and Bobby Bowden have shared throughout the decades.

11

1956'S HIGH EXPECTATIONS IN JEOPARDY

*A*fter Bowden finished the busiest year of his life, he started thinking about the 1956 football season and getting ready for its preseason camp. When he discovered that there would be more than seventy-five potential players attending camp, including seventeen members of the 1955 team, he really got excited about the new season.

His excitement quickly became contagious. Several football prognosticators, mostly associated with news services throughout the state of Georgia, declared that South Georgia had the makings of another outstanding football team and were the odds-on favorite to win their conference championship for the second year in a row.

As the excitement spread, the Williamson Rating Board jumped on the bandwagon and ranked the Tigers as one of the top ten junior college football teams in the nation.

Initially, Bowden was happy with the favorable publicity, until he realized it could quickly become a double-edged sword. Knowing the hype would either inspire his players or make them over-confident, he was afraid that if they got over-confident, they might find themselves in another Jones County fiasco.

With these thoughts racing through his mind, he began guarding his comments to the media. He didn't want to say too much, which was evident in his response to a reporter after the team's first practice. When a reporter asked him to describe his team, his only reply was, "It's going to be big and slow." He refused to elaborate or make any predictions about how he thought they would do once the season started.

According to the reporter conducting the interview, "it was easy to see that the Tigers were big," especially after seeing their team and learning that they were probably going to be fielding the largest line in the history of the Georgia Junior College Conference. Several players stood out just because of their size.

One player in particular stood out: Arthur "Tiny" Logue, a giant of a man from Mitchell, Georgia. Logue stood 6'5" tall and weighed about 335 pounds. He was a mirror image of Paul Anderson, the famous weight-lifting champion from Vidalia, Georgia, who won several medals at the Melbourne Olympic Games. Logue tried hard to emulate Anderson; when he showed up at camp, he brought a good-sized U-Haul full of weights.

Two other players dwarfed most of the others. Either of them would be considered Herculean on any college team in the 1950s. One was Richard Johnson, a 260-pound center, and the other was Foreman Miles, a 275-pound lineman. Both were all-state in high school and had transferred to South Georgia from four-year colleges. Logue, Johnson, and Miles were unquestionably the largest players on the field. However, they were not the only newcomers making an impression on the coaches. Some of the others in this category were:

Bill Schofill, a 235-pound tackle from Fort Valley, Georgia

Ed Mixon, a 205-pound guard from Cordele, Georgia

Douglas Snipes, a 195-pound guard, and military veteran, from Columbus, Georgia

Tommy Boney, a 170-pound guard from Jacksonville, Florida

Alvin Johnson, a 210-pound guard, and military veteran, from Canton, Georgia

Jimmy Grantham, a 235-pound tackle, and military veteran, from Jesup, Georgia

Winbert Lavender, a 180-pound end from Miami, Florida

Ronald Minchew, a 190-pound center from Davenport, Florida

The backfield also picked up its share of equally outstanding new talent, and some of the players in this group were:

John Robert O'Neal, a 175-pound Georiga high school all-state halfback from Valdosta, Georgia

Ralph "Buzzy" Nauright, a 175-pound Wiseman All-American halfback, and military veteran, from St. Augustine, Florida

Spencer Goad, a 185-pound Florida all-state fullback from St. Augustine, Florida

Johnnie Pichelmayer, a 180-pound halfback, and military veteran, from Birmingham, Alabama

Douglas Garrett, a 178-pound halfback, and military veteran, from Birmingham, Alabama

DeWayne "Chico" Elder, 160-pound quarterback from Stark, Florida

Lester Duncan, a 170-pound halfback from Quitman, Georgia

Verlyn Giles, a 145-pound halfback from Jacksonville, Florida

Donald Higgs, a 175-pound fullback from Lake City, Florida

Reed Hobbs, a 185-pound fullback from Jacksonville, Florida

Larry DeLoach, a 160-pound halfback from Glennville, Georgia

Jimmy Bowen, a 135-pound halfback from Waycross, Georgia

Bobby Pate, a 165-pound halfback from Fitzgerald, Georgia

Standing alone, these newcomers gave Bowden an outstanding collection of footballers to build a team from even before he started considering the seventeen returning players from the 1955 championship team.

Heading the list of the returning players were Blinkey Barber and Everett Graham. Both were big contributors to the Tigers' success in 1955, and it wasn't surprising when they picked up where they left off once practices started. Because of their consistency, Bowden selected them to be co-captains of the 1956 team.

In addition to Barber and Graham, returnees also included: Cecil Morris, Homer and Bobby Sowell, Michael Ayers, Bull Smith, Charles

Gulbrandsen, Rosby Mulkey, Lynford Wood, Fred Levy, Stumpy Franklin, Jerry Holland, Roger Wilkinson, Louis Studdard, Bobby Dixon, and Vernon Brinson.

Once these two groups combined, it was easy to see why the team was getting so much praise from preseason forecasters.

With so much talent on the field, camp quickly turned into a battle of gladiators fighting for a place on the final team. Bowden was so impressed that he decided to make camp a little more difficult—to run off any quitters.

All freshmen started the day at 6:00 a.m. and practiced for about an hour and half in shorts and T-shirts. After breakfast, around 9:30 a.m., it was back on the field in full uniform for another two hours––or longer depending on how Bowden felt at the time. This was the first of two daily practices that every candidate participated in for the first two weeks.

Typically the twice-a-day practices started with a couple of fast laps around the field followed by 10 to 15 minutes of calisthenics to warm up. Considering that temperatures reached 85 to 90 degrees by 9:00 a.m., walking two laps in full uniform probably would have sufficed.

The entire team then spent another 20 to 30 minutes walking or running through different plays and formations or running up and down the field, practicing kickoff or punt coverage. And that pretty much concluded the easy part of practice.

The real fun began with blocking and tackling drills where the primary objective seemed to be rearranging teeth. These drills usually lasted from 30 to 45 minutes, and one of the most popular exercises allowed the candidates to go head-to-head—literally. Two dummies were set up about three yards apart to create an alley or point of contact. Two players, from opposite sides of the alley, would then take turns running as hard as they could toward each other until they reached the designated point of contact between the dummies where they butted heads, under the guise of practicing their blocking and tackling skills—similar to two mountain goats ramming each other.

Another popular exercise involved ten or twelve players in a circle with another in the middle. A coach would call the name of one of the players forming the circle, and that player would run at the player in the middle and try to knock him out of the circle. The player in the middle never knew for sure where the next assault was coming from. The object, ostensibly, was to teach downfield blocking. Occasionally, two or three names were called at the same time and the player in the middle would get annihilated.

These drills were one of the main reasons football players in that era always seemed to have a black eye, bloody nose, scratched face, bruised or scraped elbow or forearm, jammed finger, twisted knees or ankles, pulled muscles, or, in some cases, concussions. All of which were pretty commonplace.

They also provided an opportunity for players to hone their more savage skills—which were not penalized as they are now. Techniques such as spearing with the helmet—usually into another player's face or chest—forearm smashing to the head or throat, chop blocking below the waist for the purpose of destroying knees and ankles, leg twisting for the same purpose, biting in a pileup, and punching or kicking another man's most valuable body parts—also usually in a pileup—were not uncommon.

After these brutal drills, players took their skills to the playing field in full-contact scrimmages. Those who survived 45 to 60 minutes of scrimmaging could then look forward to running 50, 75, or 100-yard wind sprints until they were out of breath or their legs locked up and they couldn't run any more.

Practices like these were the generally accepted format to get players ready for a season of football. They were also the primary reason coaches never knew for sure who would survive camp and be able to play once the season started. It's no wonder preseason predictions were shaky at best. South Georgia's 1956 preseason camp was no different.

Almost immediately after two-a-day practices got a little harder and competition among the players got more intense, some players decided that enduring the brutality probably wasn't in their best interest, or at least it wasn't going to be beneficial to them in the future, so they turned in their uniforms.

At the same time, Bowden laid down his expectations regarding conduct both on and off the playing field. He prohibited smoking and drinking during the season, which eliminated a few more players who were unwilling to accept these restrictions.

Separating the quitters from those with stamina was part of the idea, but when Bowden started losing key players due to injuries, the situation became a major concern. At one point, before their first game, injuries were accumulating so fast that Bowden told one reporter, "I'm beginning to believe that our toughest competition in 1956 is going to be injuries."

It's amazing just how quickly a team—or an entire season—can be thrown into disarray by a few injuries.

Before injuries demolished his team, Bowden had felt so comfortable with the number and quality of his players that he had developed two equally talented squads that he called the "purple" and "gold" teams. His idea was to use these two squads to maximize the use of his players, overcome the restrictive substitution rules, and minimize exhaustion and fatigue in the latter part of a game, which had been their Achilles' heel the year before.

He planned on starting one team, and, depending on how they were playing after a few minutes, he would either leave them in or send in the other team. He wanted to alternate the two teams continually throughout the game.

It was a concept that Coach Paul Dietzel made popular in 1958 when he used three teams—"The Chinese Bandits, The Go Team, and The White Team" at LSU to win the National Championship. Bowden came up with the idea before Dietzel used it at LSU, but he had to scrap it when South Georgia racked up injury after injury.

The most surprising season-ending injury came very early in the preseason camp when Tiny Logue, the Tigers' largest player, fractured his nose. In the '50s, injuries generally had to be life threatening, or very critical, to create concern, and no one expected Tiny's fractured nose to cause much of a problem. A busted nose was so common that most coaches and players brushed it off without a second thought. In fact, a smashed nose with a scab across it was almost expected during football season—most football players wore it as an identifying badge of honor. As it turned out, though, Tiny's nose injury was too much for him to accept because he was afraid if he got hurt again it might jeopardize his weight-lifting career.

His teammates were shocked when Logue turned in his uniform, but they were even more surprised when he asked Bowden if he could be a team manager.

In those days, a team manager was similar to today's team trainer with one major difference: a team manager in the 1950s didn't have any medical training or skills. All team managers were male students (women were not allowed) who volunteered to assist the coaches with any daily tasks the coaches felt necessary to keep the team functioning. One of their most important duties was to maintain and issue equipment. Sometimes they even wrapped an ankle or knee, or applied heating salve to a player's sore or pulled muscles—if a coach thought it was warranted. He was an important member of the team, but he wasn't a manager as the designation "team manager" might imply.

Logue's departure left the Tigers with the following forty-six players remaining on their roster:

NAME	POSITION	WEIGHT	NUMBER
Malcolm Ayers	End	180	84
Jerome "Blinkey" Barber	Fullback	180	21
Bob Barwick	Fullback	193	85
Jimmy Bowen	Halfback	135	14
Tommy Boney	Guard	175	28
Vernon Brinson	Halfback	150	11

Dewitt Chessman	End	180	60
Bobby Dixon	Fullback	185	19
Larry DeLoach	Halfback	165	21
Lester Duncan	Halfback	170	15
DeWayne "Chico" Elder	Quarterback	165	10
Billy "Stumpy" Franklin	Guard	195	24
Douglas Garrett	Halfback	175	22
Verlyn Giles	Halfback	145	2
Spencer Goad	Fullback	185	26
Everett Graham	Halfback	173	17
Charles Gulbrandsen	Tackle	220	39
Mickey Guthrie	Quarterback	175	9
David Hall	Guard	175	44
George Hersey	Halfback	160	61
Don Higgs	Fullback	178	27
Reed Hobbs	Fullback	185	81
Jerry Holland	Center	200	38
Richard Johnson	Center	260	43
Alvin Johnson	Guard	210	40
Winbert Lavender	End	186	30
Fred Levy	Guard	205	35
Foreman Miles	Tackle	276	45
Ronald Minchew	Center	180	36
Ed Mixon	Guard	210	41
Cecil Morris	End	215	34
Rosby Mulkey	Tackle	230	23
Ralph "Buzzy" Nauright	Halfback	180	29
John Robert O'Neal	Halfback	178	46
Bobby Pate	Halfback	165	18
Johnnie Pichelmayer	Halfback	180	31
Bill Schofill	Tackle	230	37
Wayne Phillips	End	170	49
Bobby Sowell	End	185	33

Homer Sowell .... End 206 25
Leeon "Bull" Smith .... End 185 13
Doug Snipes .... Guard 198 32
Louis Studdard .... Quarterback 195 20
Weyman Vickers .... Halfback 145 83
Roger Wilkinson .... Quarterback 180 12
Lynford Wood .... Tackle 210 42

It was a tough loss when Logue quit the team, but it wasn't anywhere near what the Tigers would face in the coming week. A devastating blow rocked the team when Blinkey Barber injured his right arm just days after he was selected to be one of the team's co-captains.

Initially, Barber's injury was thought to be nothing more than a bruised forearm, and because there were no medically trained personnel available to examine it, he continued practicing for the next three days with a piece of rubberized sponge taped around it. Later, after the pain and swelling got a lot worse, Bowden sent him to a local doctor to be examined.

The doctor's examination quickly revealed that his arm was broken and that it was bad enough to require a heavy cast. He restricted Blinkey from participating in any contact drills until his arm was completely healed, which, according to the doctor, would take eight to ten weeks.

Eight to ten weeks meant Barber probably wouldn't be able to play the entire season. Because he had established himself as a team leader, as well as the starting fullback, and probably the best defensive linebacker in the conference, losing him was a huge blow to the team. It was also just the beginning of a series of major setbacks.

During the same week, John Robert O'Neal, one of the team's outstanding new running backs Bowden was counting on to add more speed and depth to their backfield, tore cartilage in one of his knees. It was the type of injury that had dogged O'Neal since high school. Recovery could take anywhere from weeks to months and would require a period of rehabilitation, which effectively benched O'Neal indefinitely.

In the same week, Jimmy Bowen separated a shoulder and bruised his sternum. Although Bowen's injuries were not nearly as serious as Barber's and O'Neal's, they were bad enough to keep him on the sidelines for at least two or three weeks.

The loss of three running backs in such a short period of time not only cast a shadow on the Tigers' backfield, but it had a negative impact on the entire team.

The following week, which was the final week of practice before their first game, the Tigers faced their most devastating setback yet: Roger Wilkinson injured his back during a scrimmage. Wilkinson's injury was so serious that he was immediately hospitalized with numbness in his back and legs. The attending physician couldn't give a firm prognosis, but it was clear that there was more at stake for Wilkinson than playing football.

Wilkinson was the team's starting quarterback and Bowden had developed their offense around his skills, so his loss would have a major impact of their offensive game. He wasn't just a great quarterback though, he was a team leader and one of the best defensive backs on the team, and it was more than obvious that the defense would also be affected by his absence.

If this wasn't enough, two other important team members, Rosby Mulkey and Everett Graham were both limping, one due to a knee injury, and the other due to a sprained ankle. Neither of them had been able to practice at full speed for several days, and Bowden wasn't sure if they would be able to play in the first game.

As injuries were taking their toll on the team, a promising newcomer decided to hang up his cleats. He wasn't injured; he was in violation of a team rule. He had been smoking in the dorm, and when he got caught, Bowden took his scholarship away. It was a partial scholarship, but a scholarship nonetheless, so when he found out what his punishment was, he got upset and turned in his uniform.

It was not an easy loss for the team, but Bowden believed it was more important to enforce team rules than kowtow to bad behavior. Bowden's action sent a strong signal to the rest of the team and reinforced his players' understanding that he had set high standards for himself as well as the team—standards he had no intention of compromising.

While injuries and disciplinary problems were rapidly diluting the Tigers' high expectations for the 1956 season, not everything was gloom and doom. The last weekend of camp, before Roger Wilkinson's injury, the Tigers still found time for a little fun.

The Tigers were scheduled to play their first game against the Gordon Military Bulldog Cadets, but Bowden found out the Cadets were playing their first game the week before, and he jumped at the opportunity to do a little scouting.

Bowden was told that the Cadets' game was scheduled for 8 o'clock Saturday night in Barnesville (a small town about 40 miles south of Atlanta), so he rounded up Roger Wilkinson and Louis Studdard, the Tigers' two quarterbacks, and they left Douglas shortly after lunch on Saturday and drove the 185 miles to Barnesville.

When they got to Barnesville and found Gordon's stadium, it was almost game time, but they were surprised to find two high school teams playing in the stadium, not Gordon. Then they found out that Gordon was playing in another town.

This left them no recourse but to return to South Georgia.

Before leaving Barnesville, they stopped at a small country store on the outskirts of town to get something to eat. Wilkinson and Studdard got a cold drink and a candy bar, and Bowden got a cup of ice cream.

At the checkout counter, Bowden reached into his pocket and pulled out a handful of change. With his hand outstretched, he asked the woman behind the counter, "How much do I owe you for the ice cream?"

Without so much as a hint of a grin, the woman looked over her glasses at his outstretched hand and said, "A quarter, a dime, and a penny."

Bowden repeated "a quarter, a dime, and a penny," as he handed her the coins in that order. She turned to Wilkinson and Studdard and told them they each owed her 25 cents for their drink and candy bar.

Outside the store, Wilkinson couldn't help but comment. "Coach," he said, "I wonder why that lady didn't just tell you that you owed her 36 cents, instead of saying you owed her a quarter, a dime, and a penny."

Bowden shrugged. "You know Rog, I don't know, but I guess she must've thought I didn't look smart enough to add up that much money," he said with a grin. They laughed as they got back into the car, ribbing each other about their counting abilities.

Halfway back to Douglas, they ran into a light rain shower. By then it was dark, and as luck would have it, the windshield wipers on Bowden's old Chevy coupe wouldn't work. The rain wasn't much more than a heavy mist, but Bowden was having trouble seeing, so they debated whether they should stop and wait for the rain to pass or keep going and hope they didn't have an accident. While they were considering their options and looking for a place to pull off the road, Wilkinson told Bowden that he thought he could reach up under the dashboard and manually move the wipers' rocker arm. If the wipers moved like he thought they would, they could keep going.

Bowden thought it was worth a shot, so Wilkinson got down on the front floorboard on the passenger side of the car and found the wiper rocker arm under the dashboard. He moved the arm back and forth, and sure enough, the windshield wipers swished and Bowden was able to see again.

As Wilkinson worked the wipers, they continued on their merry way for the next few minutes until the sky opened up and the rain really started coming down. Bowden yelled to Wilkinson, "Faster! Faster, Roger! I can't see Rog! Faster, faster!"

Roger, on the floorboards, got to work and, with Bowden's encouragement, was able to keep the wipers moving fast enough for them to creep along until the rain stopped.

When they finally got back to South Georgia, some of Wilkinson's teammates heard about the windshield wiper episode, and they couldn't resist kidding him about it, saying he shouldn't worry about keeping his starting position after his performance. Of course they didn't know that two days later an injury would remove him from the starting lineup.

The day after Wilkinson got hurt, four days before their opening game, Bowden tried to measure the impact their losses would have on the team. Wilkinson's loss was the most critical because their offense had been developed around his skills, and neither of their backup quarterbacks had ever started a game at South Georgia.

His second biggest concern was the defense. Both Wilkinson and Barber, who played cornerback and linebacker, were two of the team's best and most dependable defensive players, and Bowden had been counting on both of them to lead the defense. They were just two players, but he couldn't help but believe their loss was going to have a huge impact.

After a couple of restless nights, he finally decided that shuffling players around or trying to make major changes at the last minute would probably disrupt the team even more, so he cautiously announced their starting lineup.

That lineup included:

Left end	CecilMorris	215 pounds	sophomore
Left tackle	Foreman Miles	276 pounds	sophomore
Left guard	Stumpy Franklin	195 pounds	sophomore
Center	Richard Johnson	260 pounds	sophomore
Right guard	Fred Levy	205 pounds	sophomore
Right tackle	Charles Gulbrandsen.	220 pounds	sophomore
Right end	Homer Sowell	206 pounds	sophomore
Quarterback	Louis Studdard	195 pounds	sophomore

Right halfback..Everett Graham......... 173 pounds ... sophomore
Fullback ....Bobby Dixon .... 185 pounds ... sophomore
Left halfback ....Larry Deloach .... 165 pounds ... sophomore

If it was decided later that Graham wasn't able to start because of his ankle injury, Johnnie Pichelmayer, a freshman, would start at right halfback.

On September 29, the reigning conference champions arrived in Barnesville with a team that had been reduced to thirty-five players—most of whom were hurting and would be playing with some sort of injury. Thirty-five was far less than either Bowden or Gibson had anticipated they would start the season with just three weeks earlier.

Their diminished numbers, all the preseason hype, and the inquiring eyes of sports writers gave the Tigers an abnormal amount of pre-game jitters and butterflies.

South Georgia Tigers vs Gordon Military Cadets

As soon as the Tigers took the opening kickoff, Bowden's worst nightmares were realized. On their first series of plays, several players lost their cool and played like a bunch of out-of-control hotheads, which kept them moving backward instead of forward as the penalty yards multiplied. On their first fourth down, they had to punt from deep inside their own territory, but the punt was blocked and recovered by Gordon on the Tigers' 23-yard line.

To make matters worse, another penalty was called against the Tigers, and the ball was moved very close to their goal line. Three plays later, the Cadets sashayed into the end zone scoring the first touchdown of the contest. After converting the point-after-touchdown, the Cadets took a very quick and surprising 7-0 lead.

Even though the Tigers had more than three and a half quarters to regain control of the game, they started playing with an unmistakable sense of desperation. The Cadets, on the other hand, were jumping for joy.

The Cadets' jubilation caused confusion on the field, which helped South Georgia come back to tie the score. Johnnie Pichelmayer returned the Cadets kickoff to the Tigers' 45-yard line, and on their first play from scrimmage, DeWayne Elder, who had replaced Studdard at quarterback, slipped through the line of scrimmage and sprinted 55 yards for the score.

Under normal circumstances, the quick recovery should have calmed the Tigers down some and put them in a more controlled state of mind. However, it seemed to have the opposite effect, because they started playing like they were in a dogfight, instead of a football game, and their recklessness kept them backpedaling after each penalty was called.

Midway through the second quarter, while the score was still tied, a South Georgia defensive lineman broke through the Cadets' offensive line and could have easily sacked their quarterback for a big loss. Instead, he grabbed the quarterback by the back of his shoulder pads and pounded his back—it was a senseless, unprovoked, ridiculous act, and he did it right in front of a game official. The Tiger player was immediately ejected from the game, and the Tigers received another 15-yard penalty.

The incident went a long way in helping the Cadets score another seven points. And even though the Tigers got lucky and managed to pull within one point of tying the score before the first half ended, they never stopped being their own worst enemy.

At halftime, Bowden and Gibson tried desperately to calm their players down and make them aware of the damage the outrageous mistakes were causing their team. Their words, however, fell on deaf ears, and the team played the second half the same way they'd played the first. Gordon easily took control of the second half, scored 14 more points, and won the game by a score of 28–13.

Dismayed and embarrassed, Bowden told reporters after the game, "We lost because we were outplayed, out-passed, out-conditioned, and out-coached." He didn't have to say anything about the score; it was on the scoreboard for everyone to see. "It hurts anytime you lose," he said, "but it really hurts bad when you lose the way we did tonight."

On the way home, the Tigers couldn't stop asking themselves, "How could we have fallen so far so fast from everyone's preseason expectations?" It was more than obvious that their high preseason expectations were in jeopardy.

12

SEARCHING FOR A SOLUTION

*E*ven *before they got back* to Douglas, Bowden was already thinking about what he needed to do to get his team back on a winning track. After losing to Gordon, he was determined to start over and live up to preseason expectations.

Despite the large number of injuries, he believed this team had enough experience and raw talent among their healthy players to win any of their games if he prepared and motivated them properly. Like always, he felt he was the one most responsible for the way the team played, whether they won or lost.

Once they got home, he and Gibson decided their biggest problems were mental rather than physical. They knew that playing aggressively was important and they didn't want to discourage aggressiveness, but they also knew they had to make sure that every player understood that when he lost his composure and played like an out-of-control lunatic, the whole team suffered.

They were confident that adjustments could be made before the next game because they were sure the team was embarrassed enough by what happened in Barnesville to not want to repeat their performance against the Cadets.

Throughout the next week, they continually emphasized the importance of playing together, controlling tempers, and avoiding stupid mistakes. At the same time, they made three changes in their starting lineup.

The first change was to move DeWayne Elder into the starting quarterback position ahead of Louis Studdard. Most Tiger offensive plays started from a split-T formation that required the quarterback to run with the football; therefore, Elder was the logical choice since Studdard was more of a drop-back passer. Bowden started working Bobby Pate into the position as well, in case they needed more depth later in the season.

Bowden was also able to get Everett Graham and Rosby Mulkey back in the game now that their injuries had healed.

South Georgia Tigers vs West Georgia Braves

AFTER MAKING NECESSARY ADJUSTMENTS, Bowden and Gibson were confident they were ready for their first home game against the West Georgia Braves.

When game time arrived Saturday night, October 7, the Tigers were wearing new uniforms: white jerseys, purple numbers, silver pants, and gold helmets. For the first time in the history of South Georgia football, their helmets had face guards. They were nothing like the birdcage-style face guards of today, but a single plastic or Plexiglas bar that ran from one side of the helmet to the other in front of the player's mouth.

Whether it was their new uniforms, new face guards, or the fact that they were playing on their home field, they seemed much more at ease and self-assured than the week before, and they were rocking and rolling as soon as Larry DeLoach took the opening kickoff. Three plays later, Elder faded back behind Stumpy Franklin, Charles Gulbrandsen, and Bobby Sowell and arched a beautiful 25-yard pass to DeLoach who was wide open, running down the right side of the field. Once DeLoach grabbed the ball, he galloped untouched into pay dirt for the game's first touchdown.

The pace of the game slowed considerably until the Tigers got busy again late in the quarter and forced a Braves' fumble at their own 30-yard line. When the loose ball hit the ground, Stumpy Franklin pounced on it for the Tigers just as time ran out in the first quarter.

As the second quarter started, Everett Graham picked up 20 yards. Two plays later, Bobby Dixon charged across the goal line scoring the Tigers' second TD. The Tigers were in front of the Braves by 12 points early in the second quarter.

South Georgia's domination continued when Cecil Morris broke through the Braves' offensive line and lowered the boom on their quarterback, who let the ball slip out of his hands. As soon as it hit the ground, Rosby Mulky was there to smother it for the Tigers at the mid-field marker.

Once the Tigers took possession of the ball again, Doug Garrett picked up 10 yards. Then Elder raced for another 15 before Graham high-stepped it across the goal line from 25 yards out for the Tigers' third touchdown. The point-after-touchdown gave the Tigers a comfortable 19-point lead just before the first half ended.

In the third quarter, the Tigers' juggernaut forced the Braves to punt the football for the fifth time. This time their kick went out-of-bounds at their 42-yard line.

Elder, DeLoach, Graham, and Dixon relentlessly chipped away at the Braves' defense, picking up short, productive gains until they moved the ball to the 3-yard line. Once they reached the 3-yard line, Elder leaped over the goal line to score their fourth TD. Homer Sowell converted the extra point, and the Tigers led by 26 points.

Toward the end of the fourth quarter, West Georgia put together their first and only serious threat of the contest. Using a slow and somewhat conservative ground attack, they moved the football from their own 30-yard line to the Tigers' 23.

Once they got within what they thought was striking distance of the Tigers' goal line, they changed their strategy and started throwing the football. This turned out to be a serious mistake because Bobby Pate, an ever-alert defender, grabbed their first pass at the 10-yard line, killing their last chance of putting any points on the scoreboard.

Although fewer than two minutes remained in the game when the interception occurred, the Tigers didn't stop trying to increase their lead. As the final minutes ticked away, Elder rifled a short, flat pass to Winbert Lavender at the 19-yard line. Once Lavender got the ball under control, he lateraled it back to Jimmy Bowen, who scrambled for another 39 yards before being driven out-of-bounds at the Braves' 42-yard line. Two plays later, the game ended just as the Tigers reached the Braves' 20-yard line.

South Georgia rushed for 229 yards and passed for 97 compared to West Georgia's 139 yards rushing and 23 yards passing. The only downsides to South Georgia's game, according to Bowden, were the continuing mistakes that resulted in needless penalties. Penalties cost them 80 yards compared to the 10 West Georgia lost.

South Georgia Tigers vs Middle Georgia Wolverines

Preparing for their game against the Middle Georgia Wolverines, the Tigers primarily worked on timing and execution and spent a lot of time trying to break bad habits.

Bowden knew they couldn't continue making the same mistakes and expect to win. He wanted the problem fixed before their next game against the Wolverines, who had already won their first two games.

In the midst of the pressure, Bowden got some good news: Roger Wilkinson was released by his doctor and allowed to return to the team. He was still suffering with some soreness and back pain, but his doctor gave him the okay to participate in light workouts with the understanding that he wouldn't participate in any contact drills until his back stopped hurting completely. Even with these restrictions, Wilkinson's unexpected return reenergized the Tigers.

On October 14, the Tigers and the Wolverines squared off against each other at South Georgia's College Field before a larger-than-normal crowd of avid, cheering South Georgia fans. The size of the crowd, and the enthusiasm and excitement they displayed, motivated the already electrified Tigers, so much so that when the game got underway, the Wolverines were powerless to stop them from scoring the first touchdown.

Doug Garrett opened the game with a beautiful demonstration of open-field running when he returned the kickoff to the Wolverines' 47-yard line.

The excited crowd was then treated to a huge surprise as Roger Wilkinson trotted onto the field. His return got the people on their feet in a standing ovation. Two plays later, Wilkinson looped a short swing pass to Bobby Pate, who weaved his way to the 19-yard-line.

On the next play, Pate relit the crowd's excitement as he circled his right end, twisted away from a would-be-tackler, and charged into the end zone scoring the first touchdown of the game. Homer Sowell bisected the uprights and South Georgia took a very quick 7-point lead.

The quickness of the score added fuel to the already fired-up Tigers. When they kicked off to the Wolverines, a herd of tacklers, led by Ed Mixon and Tommy Boney, stampeded downfield and slammed their runner to the ground at their 18-yard line.

The Tigers' defense wasted no time, immediately dominating the Wolverines offense and forcing a fumble around their own 10-yard line. A wild scramble for the dropped ball caused it to be knocked into the end zone, and that's where Bull Smith pounced on it for another Tiger 6-pointer. Elder converted the extra point, and South Georgia upped their lead to 14 points while the game was still early in the first quarter.

When South Georgia kicked off again, their unyielding defense dismantled the Wolverines' offense and forced them to resort to punting the football from deep inside their own territory. Their botched punt wobbled out-of-bounds around their own 43-yard line.

As soon as South Georgia regained possession of the ball at the Wolverines' 43-yard line, Elder, Pate, Graham, and Spencer Goad went to work, pushing the line of scrimmage down the field. At the Wolverines' 5-yard line, a bad exchange between Elder and Richard Johnson caused a Tiger fumble and derailed what had been another sure touchdown for Tigers.

It was the kind of turnover that frequently changes a game's momentum, but this time, the Tigers were determined that they were not going to be affected or discouraged. Their determination stopped the Wolverines' from moving the football beyond the 20-yard line, forcing them to punt from deep inside their own territory again.

Johnnie Pichelmayer grabbed the punt at the 50-yard line and took off running toward the left side of the field. Seconds later, as the Wolverines' downfield coverage converged on him, he lateral passed the ball back to Doug Garrett who was running in the opposite direction. The perfectly executed double reverse helped Garrett break free and get to the Wolverines' 30-yard line.

Stumpy Franklin and Lynford Wood kept the Tigers rolling by opening a big hole in the right side of the Wolverines' defense. Pichelmayer sprinted through and raced into the end zone, scoring the Tigers' third TD. Homer Sowell converted the extra point, and the Tigers took a 20-0 lead just as the first half ended.

In the locker room, after Bowden realized they'd played an almost errorless game, he allowed himself to hope they'd found the solution to their problem.

His hope, however, deteriorated almost immediately after the second half got underway.

It was hard for him to believe that the team that took the field after halftime was the same team that had dominated the game only minutes earlier. South Georgia struggled just to maintain their lead throughout the second half.

The same old problem tormented them, and penalties in the second half not only helped the Wolverines score a safety and a touchdown, they also kept the Tigers from adding any points to their own score. "Because of the way we played in the second half, we were darn lucky to win," Bowden said after the game. He was thankful for their win, but it was obvious he was disappointed with his team's performance when he told reporters, "Our players made so many inexcusable mistakes in the second half that they looked like a completely different team than the one that played the first half."

Bowden and Gibson both described their team's play in the second half as "pathetic" and stated that, except for the performance of Pate, Mulkey, and Mixon, who kept the team from being run completely off the field in the second half, there was nothing to brag about.

Statistically, the offensive game was almost even, with the Tigers picking up 25 more yards on the ground than the Wolverines. However, second-half mistakes cost the Tigers 85 yards in penalties, eliminating any advantage their ground game had given them.

Bowden and Gibson couldn't understand why their players were continuing to make the same costly mistakes over and over again in every game.

The situation had gotten so far out of hand that Bowden considered it their biggest problem—even bigger than having key players unable to play because of injuries.

Initially, he thought the problem would be simple to correct. But now, as penalty yards continued to multiply, he realized that finding a solution wasn't going to be as easy as he first thought.

It was around this time that Bowden started using the word "Dadgumit" a lot more than he had in the past. Using the word for emphasis, he would say something like, "Now, dadgumit, boys, you're going to have to stay onside or you're going to defeat yourselves," or "Now listen to me, dadgumit, here's what we've got to do if we want to beat this team." To many people, dadgumit might have sounded like idle slang, but it didn't take the players long to learn that when Bowden said, "dadgumit," they better pay close attention to what he was saying.

He was ready to do more than just use dadgumit to stress that football was as much a mental game as it was a physical one, and that they needed to start thinking about what they were doing.

At first he thought he would just pull the offending player out of the game. But, he realized that plan could quickly become counterproductive if he had to pull several first-team players off the field at the same time, so he decided to punish the guilty players by giving them extra work at practice. Extra work to Bowden meant running more laps before practice, or more wind sprints after practice. Running, he thought, would give the players a little more incentive to grasp the importance of correcting the penalty problem. Even though it was less than an ultimatum, the players being punished would probably think it was an ultimatum before they got through running.

According to some of Bowden's former players, for the next few days, practice was the toughest it had been all season. Most of the offending players had to crawl off the field after running wind sprints because they couldn't get to their feet.

For some reason, though, this punishment didn't last more than a couple of days before Bowden stopped it.

Some players believe Bowden stopped it because he felt sorry for some of the players being punished. Others argue that the only reason the running stopped was because Bowden assumed he had made his point. Heading into their next game against the Troy State Trojans, Bowden could only hope the problem had been corrected and his players were ready.

Troy State was a four-year college, but Bowden and Gibson both felt confident they could win the game if their players played smart football for sixty minutes.

South Georgia Tigers vs Troy State Trojans

ON OCTOBER 21, the South Georgia Tigers and the Troy State Trojans squared off in Troy, Alabama, in what many former South Georgia players remember as the toughest game they ever played.

Difficult weather conditions that night made playing football almost impossible. Throughout the game, intermittent downpours and light showers made the field look more like a lake than a football field. The football, once it was wet, which was immediate, was almost impossible to control and was frequently dropped. Passing wasn't even a consideration. From the opening kickoff until the final whistle, it was a game either team could have won—or lost—depending on the bounce of the ball and the depth of the water on the field.

The game got underway when Everett Graham returned the Trojans' kickoff to the Tigers' 33-yard line. After that, the game turned into a brawl in a mud pit. On the Tigers first play from scrimmage, Larry DeLoach attempted to run off tackle with the football, but because of the field's condition, he slipped and slid so much that he lost control of the ball when he was hammered behind the line by at least a half dozen Trojans. When a gang of Trojans piled on top of the loose football at the 28-yard line, it looked like the Tigers were swimming backward.

A couple plays later, Troy discovered just how hard the weather made it to hold onto the football when they returned the favor of a fumble back to the Tigers on the 20-yard line.

Getting control of the football again could have given the Tigers a big break had they not been penalized 15 yards and pushed back to their 5-yard line on the next play. Not only did the penalty push them deeper into the mud hole, it made Bowden realize that the problem he had hoped was resolved was still very much alive and well.

Because the Tigers were unable to move the football any farther away from their goal line than the 5-yard line, they were quickly forced into a precarious fourth down punting situation. Their punter had to stand closer to the line of scrimmage than normal and hurry his kick. But when he hurried his kick, he slipped on the wet grass and the ball fluttered out-of-bounds at the 26-yard line.

The Trojans again had control of the football close to the Tigers' goal line. This time they were able to capitalize on the Tigers' mistakes and score the first TD of the contest. After converting the PAT, they took a 7-point lead.

South Georgia had played the first eight minutes of the game with their backs against their own goal line, trying to stop a much larger team in the worst weather and field conditions imaginable. For the rest of the first quarter, and most of the second, the two teams played toe-to-toe in an evenly matched conflict in which neither team was able to maintain control of the ball long enough to score any more points.

In the latter part of the second quarter, South Georgia started from their 30-yard line and managed to put together their best drive of the night. DeWayne Elder called the plays, and Everett Graham, Bobby Dixon, and Spencer Goad carried the mail. The three running backs trudged through rain, mud, and the Trojans' defense until they finally got inside their opponent's 15-yard line.

By then, the muddy conditions were beginning to take their toll, and the Tigers found themselves in a fourth down situation needing at least 2 yards to keep their drive alive. Knowing the game clock was ticking off the last few minutes of the first half, Bowden opted to go for the first down instead of trying a field goal, hoping to even the score before the half ended.

With their hopes riding on this one play, Goad charged straight ahead trying to pick up the needed 2 yards, but because of the wet ground and his weary legs, he slipped and came up short. The football went back to the Trojans.

Disappointed, but not discouraged enough to quit, the Tigers stopped the Trojans dead in their tracks and forced them to punt on fourth down. But their kicker never had a chance as Bill Schofill and Richard Johnson vaulted the defense and tackled him in the end zone for a safety.

Shortly after that, the first half ended, with South Georgia trailing Troy by a score of 7-2.

The second half echoed the first; both teams had to depend almost entirely on their defenses to stay competitive. However, late in the third quarter, Troy recovered a South Georgia fumble and the Tigers were assessed two consecutive 15-yard penalties. The penalties gave Troy a first down inside the Tigers' 15-yard line and the encouragement they needed to score their second touchdown.

That second touchdown ended up being the final score of the game, giving Troy a 13–2 victory over a very determined group of South Georgia players.

Even though the record books show that Troy won the game, it would be hard for anyone who saw the game to argue that the South Georgia Tigers didn't outplay the much larger Trojans. The Tigers could have easily been victorious if they had not fumbled the ball three times and received several critical penalties.

The loss was hard for Bowden to accept, but he couldn't be unhappy about the way his players stood up to a four-year college team, or the way their starting linemen, who played almost 60 minutes in the worst imaginable weather conditions, kept fighting until the end.

Statistically, the Tigers gained 154 yards rushing compared to Troy's' 120 yards, and they led the Trojans in first downs 10 to 5. Unfortunately, they also led them in fumbles 3 to 1, and in penalties, where they lost 95 yards compared to Troy's 60.

Although the game was played in difficult weather conditions, Bowden knew that neither the weather nor their opponent gave his players as much trouble as their own mistakes. "The final score would have been a lot different if we hadn't made so many mental mistakes," he said.

South Georgia Tigers vs Jacksonville State Gamecocks

BOWDEN WAS DISAPPOINTED after the Troy game. He couldn't figure out why his boys continued to be their own toughest opponents. The team's weaknesses made it difficult for him to feel optimistic about their next game against the Jacksonville State Gamecocks, another four-year college team that had already won all six of their games.

Bowden knew the Gamecocks would be ready to play at the top of their game. Not only was the match scheduled to be played on their home field, it was their last home game of the season. He expected that the Gamecocks would be their toughest opponent of the year.

To compound their situation, the Tigers lost another key player in the Troy game to injury when Richard Johnson, their big center, was sidelined with a serious sprained ankle.

In addition, Bowden was still wrestling with the idea of starting Roger Wilkinson in the game. If he played Wilkinson, there was a chance he might re-injure his back and be out for the rest of the year. If Bowden didn't play him, Wilkinson would have another week to recuperate and would probably be ready to start the following week against Georgia Military College, when the conference championship would be at stake.

He wrestled with the question all week but didn't decide until the day before the game, while they were traveling to Jacksonville, to start DeWayne Elder at quarterback.

Knowing that they were going into their toughest contest of the season without key players against a team eager to please their fans at home, and that they still hadn't found a solution to their penalties problem, it was hard for the team not to simply look past it and onto their game against GMC.

As a consequence, when the game got underway on October 28, it was evident almost immediately that it was going to be a long, rough night for the outmatched Tigers.

Things began to fall apart right after the opening kickoff when the Tigers were forced to punt from deep inside their own territory. Once the ball was kicked, Cecil Morris raced down field and put a brutal tackle on the Gamecocks' punt returner. The impact was so severe that both Morris and the Jacksonville player were knocked unconscious. Some of the Tigers said even they saw stars.

Tommy Johns, one of the Tigers' team managers, ran onto the field to see if Morris was okay. As soon as he got to where Morris was stretched out on the field, he turned right around and raced back to the sideline where Bowden was standing. Breathing deeply, all he could say was, "Coach, his mouth and eyes are wide open, but he's not making a sound."

Johns tries to make light of it today, saying, "He was just lying on his back, smiling and staring at the stars over Alabama." But at the time, seeing Morris lying there, eyes and mouth wide open with blood oozing from a gash in his forehead, he couldn't help thinking Morris might be dead. He said the cut on Morris's forehead was so bad "the skin was peeled back," and he could "see his skull."

Bowden asked the officials to stop the game and call an ambulance. In those days, an ambulance wasn't always standing by on the field as it is today.

Once the ambulance arrived, Bowden instructed Johns to go with Morris to the hospital and stay with him until he could pick them up after the game. The hospital was in Anniston, Alabama, about forty miles away.

After Morris was removed from the field, the game resumed and the Tigers managed to hold the Gamecocks and force them to punt after their first series of downs. This was the last time the Tigers were able to feel good about their performance in the game.

On their first offensive play from the line of scrimmage, Elder dropped back and threw a down-and-out pass to Homer Sowell, but as the pass was released, one of the Gamecocks' defensive backs stepped in front of Sowell, intercepted the pass, and ran it back across the goal line, scoring the first touchdown of the game. After converting the extra point, the Gamecocks took a 7-point lead.

The Tigers somehow kept the Gamecocks from scoring again in the first quarter, but it was obvious they had ruffled their feathers because as soon as the second quarter started, the Gamecocks turned up the pressure, and the Tigers started dropping the football like it was a hot potato. Jacksonville capitalized on almost every Tiger turnover, scoring three touchdowns before the half ended.

At the start of the second half, the Tigers made a gallant effort to get back in the game, but every time they seemed to be making some progress, or they got close enough to Jacksonville's goal line to be a threat, they either fumbled the football or threw an interception.

They continued handing the ball to the Gamecocks in the second half, making it easy for Jacksonville to score three more touchdowns and win the game 40-0.

Roger Wilkinson played sporadically, but even that wasn't enough to make much of a difference.

Using just about every player on their bench, the Gamecocks rushed for 225 yards and passed for another 85 yards, while the Tigers struggled to pick up 100 yards rushing and 47 yards passing. To help advance the Gamecocks cause, the struggling Tigers turned the football over at least six times.

After the game, Bowden conceded that they were beaten by a better team. "This was the first time we were beaten without beating ourselves," Bowden said.

It was also the first game in which they received fewer penalties than their opponent. They were only penalized 35 yards, which made Bowden hope they were finished with unnecessary penalties for the rest of the season.

Once they were on the buses, the team headed to Anniston to pick up Johns and Morris. When they arrived at the hospital, Johns told Bowden that the doctor who had "sewed up Morris's head" suggested that he be admitted to the hospital for observation for at least twenty-four hours. Johns said Bowden looked at him incredulously and said, "We can't just leave him in the hospital. We've got to get him back to Douglas and get ready for our next game."

Johns and a couple of Morris's teammates helped Morris to the bus, and they departed Anniston for South Georgia.

Johns doesn't remember if Morris played their next game or not, but he does remember that he laid in the back of the bus with an ice pack on his head, moaning and groaning most of the way back to Douglas.

13

GETTING BACK TO
PRESEASON EXPECTATIONS

On the way home from Alabama, Bowden had plenty of time to think about their next game and the physical condition of all of his players. Morris's injury was just one more he could add to a long list that had been plaguing this team since the start of the season. Almost every player in the starting lineup was suffering from some sort of injury.

After giving it a lot of thought, Bowden decided to change their practices from the customary rough contact drills and daily scrimmages, to much lighter workouts with very little contact.

Non-contact practices were almost unheard-of in the 1950s. Most coaches believed that football players had to be able to play with a few minor injuries and through a little pain or they probably weren't worth keeping on the team.

Georgia Tech's coach, Bobby Dodd, was one of the few coaches who didn't totally accept the reigning philosophy and wasn't afraid to deviate from it. But since playing with injuries was generally expected, none of Bowden's players ever expected they would see anything different at South Georgia. That is until the next Monday morning when some of them overheard Bowden tell a local sports reporter, "Our boys have the ability to win every week if they're healthy, but right now they're pretty banged up, so we'll be conducting light workouts all week."

Once Bowden recognized that an accumulation of minor injuries could be a problem, he wasn't afraid to break from the "norm" to do what he thought was best.

For the rest of the week, practices were vastly different from anything the Tigers had ever seen.

South Georgia Tigers vs Georgia Military Bulldogs

ON NOVEMBER 4, while the Tigers were warming up before their game with GMC, Bowden noticed that his players seemed more upbeat than normal and more eager than usual for the game to get started. He hoped his decision to change practice was having a positive impact.

His hope, however, was quickly challenged when the Tigers fumbled the opening kickoff and the Bulldogs recovered it. It looked like their opponent was about to take control of the game without even breaking a sweat.

While Bowden was having flashbacks of their first game of the season against Gordon, his players—who had endured playing two tough four-year college teams in a row—had no intention of letting an early fumble weaken their determination to win this game. And, to convey that message to their opponent, Homer Sowell and Bull Smith blitzed the Bulldogs' quarterback on the first play from scrimmage.

The blitz and a 15-yard penalty pushed the Bulldogs back to their own 41-yard line in two plays. After their 24-yard loss, the Bulldogs offense quick kicked the football on third down—apparently to avoid losing any more yards.

After the quick kick, the Tigers started their first series of downs on offense from their own 20-yard line. Roger Wilkinson, who was now playing full-time, and Everett Graham moved the ball back to the 44-yard line in three plays. Wilkinson then dropped back and rifled a sizzling pass to Homer Sowell for 19 more yards.

The play moved the Tigers across mid-field and into the Bulldog end of the field. Wilkinson, Graham, and DeLoach's collaboration kept the ball moving closer to the Bulldogs' goal line until DeLoach broke loose from 18 yards out and outran the entire Bulldog secondary into pay dirt. Homer Sowell converted the extra point, and the Tigers took a 7-0 lead.

The Bulldogs weren't ready to give up, though, and they came clawing back and scored their own 6 points before the end of the first quarter.

In the beginning of the second quarter, both teams used short ground gains and alternating defenses to keep the score close, until the Tigers got to the Bulldogs' 35-yard line and got a little more adventurous with their offense.

Wilkinson unleashed another well-aimed pass to Homer Sowell, who had gotten free in the end zone, giving the Tigers their second touchdown. Sowell also kicked the PAT, and the Tigers went ahead of the Bulldogs 14-6.

In the third quarter, the Bulldogs were forced to punt from deep inside their own territory. The short punt landed the Tigers at their own 48-yard line.

Graham and DeLoach went back to work and quickly moved the ball to the Bulldogs' 19-yard line. From there, Wilkinson lofted a short looping pass to Spencer Goad, and Goad charged across the goal line for another Tiger TD.

In the final quarter, the Tigers' persistence and determination really started to pay off. They scored 3 more touchdowns and 19 more points before the final whistle sounded.

The onslaught started when Tommy Boney broke through the Bulldogs' protective wall and hit one of their running backs head-on. The runner dropped the football, and Winbert Lavender came up with it for the Tigers.

After that, Louis Studdard, who had replaced Wilkinson at quarterback, lateraled the ball to Bobby Pate who carried it to the Bulldogs' 20-yard line. Bobby Dixon picked up another 7 yards, and from the Bulldogs' 13-yard line, Doug Garrett brought the drive to a climax when he zigzagged his way into pay dirt for the Tigers' fourth touchdown. The Tigers were looking good at 26-6.

After another Bulldog punt, the Tigers had the ball on their 35-yard line. From there, Chico Elder, at quarterback for Studdard, ran an option play and pitched the ball to Jimmy Bowen. Bowen turned upfield and outran several Bulldog tacklers for 60 yards until he crossed the 5-yard line. When he crossed the 5-yard line, he slowly circled back toward his teammates, thinking he had scored, and was tackled by a pursuing defender.

The Tigers lined up on the Bulldogs' 5-yard line, and Bowen carried the ball to the 1-yard line before Elder called his own number and dove into the end zone behind Jerry Holland and Tommy Boney. The Tigers had their fifth touchdown and were ahead of the Bulldogs 32-6.

In a few short plays, the Bulldogs were forced to punt again. When the Tigers got the football, it was late in the final quarter, but their running backs weren't ready to stop showing their heels to the Bulldogs. Starting from their own 25-yard line, Lester Duncan, Bobby Dixon, and Larry DeLoach alternated moving the football downfield until DeLoach darted into the end zone from 5 yards out for their sixth touchdown. Elder booted the PAT and the Tigers took home a very impressive 39-6 victory over Georgia Military College.

The win made the Tigers' conference record three wins to one loss and kept their hopes of winning the conference championship alive. It also resolved any doubts Bowden harbored about the previous week's practice.

In his first full-time performance since being injured, Wilkinson completed six aerials for an average of 23 yards per pass and ran for 29 more yards on the ground. He was also credited with breaking up two Bulldog passes and assisting on at least nine tackles for the defense.

Larry DeLoach led South Georgia's running game by scoring 2 touchdowns and rushing for 87 yards.

This was the first game of the 1956 season in which South Georgia cleared its bench and utilized every member of the squad. It was also the first and only game the Tigers played all season in which penalties were not a factor. By the end of the game, neither team had been penalized more than 15 yards.

After another conference victory, the South Georgians returned home, excited by their win, but subdued by the thought that they still had two very important conference games ahead of them.

South Georgia Tigers vs Middle Georgia Wolverines

JUST FIVE DAYS AFTER DEFEATING the GMC Bulldogs, the Tigers journeyed to Cochran, Georgia, for another tilt against the Middle Georgia Wolverines. This was the same team they had dominated in the first half of their previous game, but struggled against in the second half, barely clinging to the big lead they built up in the first half.

Remembering their first game and the way the Bulldogs had played in the second half, Bowden wasn't completely confident they could beat the Wolverines the second time.

It had always been his opinion that playing a team for a second time, especially if the team had lost, was particularly difficult. He knew the Wolverines would be looking to avenge their earlier defeat, and they'd be playing on their home field, giving them extra incentive. On top of it all, the game was scheduled for Thursday instead of Saturday, giving the Tigers less practice time.

By Thursday afternoon, when South Georgia arrived in Cochran, Bowden and Gibson's confidence was beginning to creep back. Even with only a short week to get ready, they were encouraged by their players' improved attitude and enthusiasm. They also knew the Tigers were in better shape, physically and mentally, than they had been all season.

When they arrived in Cochran, one thing immediately caught

their attention: it was definitely football weather in middle Georgia. The sky was gray and overcast, the temperature was in the mid-fifties, and there was a cool breeze blowing. By game time, the temperature was supposed to drop to the forties, and by evening, it would be below freezing. It was at least twenty degrees cooler in Cochran than it was in Douglas.

At eight that evening, while the temperature was hovering around the 40-degree mark, the team captains met in the center of the field for the coin toss. The Wolverines won and elected to receive. It was the first coin toss the Tigers had lost all season, and some South Georgia fans couldn't help but think it was a bad sign.

But, after the Wolverines received the opening kickoff, the Tigers shackled their running game immediately, forcing them to attempt a quick pass over the middle of the line on third down.

The pass might have been successful if it hadn't been for the Tigers' middle linebacker, Fred Levy, who stepped in front of their intended receiver and grabbed the football. Levy was immediately smothered at the 38-yard line, but his interception put the Tigers in an ideal position to mount a successful drive.

From the Wolverines' 38-yard line, Bobby Dixon, Everett Graham, and Bobby Pate banged out enough yardage to move the football to the 8-yard line in three plays. On their next play, Graham charged through the line of scrimmage and into the Wolverines' end zone for the Tigers' first score. Homer Sowell kicked the extra point, and the Tigers took a 7-0 lead before they'd been on the field five minutes.

For the remainder of the first quarter and into the second, neither team seemed capable of developing enough consistency in their offense to be a threat to their opponent. But, midway through the second quarter, the Tigers finally started moving the ball with some regularity.

The Tigers mounted a slow, methodical drive in which Dixon was the designated workhorse. Starting from their own 35-yard line, he gained 6, 16, 4, and 8 yards respectively, moving the ball to the Wolverines' 31-yard line.

Once they reached the Wolverines' 31, Wilkinson executed a perfect fake handoff to Graham before bootlegging it around his right end and racing across the goal line for the Tigers' second touchdown. At the half, South Georgia had a 13-point lead.

Halfway through the third quarter, Graham sprinted around his left end, twisted away from one would-be-tackler and galloped 54 yards for another Tiger 6-pointer.

The Wolverines stayed at zero until shortly after the fourth quarter got underway when they capitalized on a Tiger fumble, scoring their only touchdown of the game.

In the closing minutes of the contest, the Wolverines started throwing the football in a desperate attempt to close the gap on the scoreboard. It seemed to be working for a couple of plays—until Wilkinson sabotaged their last real threat when he intercepted one of their passes.

Taking advantage of the momentum shift, Wilkinson unloaded a beautiful 30-yard bomb to Graham, who grabbed the ball while running free down the right side of the field. Once he had the football under control, Graham kicked his stride into overdrive and outran the entire Wolverine secondary, scoring the Tigers' fourth touchdown. Homer Sowell's PAT was the final point scored in the contest, and it gave the Tigers a very important 26-7 victory over the Middle Georgia Wolverines.

To defeat the Middle Georgia clan for the second time in the 1956 season, the Tigers played nearly flawless football for four quarters, with standout defensive play by Jerry Holland and Stumpy Franklin. Holland pestered the Wolverines' offense all night, repeatedly stopping their ball carriers for little or no gain. Stumpy, more often than not, was in the Wolverines' backfield disrupting their plays and knocking their runners on their behinds. Holland and Franklin stood out, but the rest of the Tigers' defense also played an outstanding game, limiting Middle Georgia to a grand total of 71 yards rushing on offense.

The offensive line also had a solid game. By protecting their passer and opening large holes in their opponent's defense, they made it possible for the offense to pick up 224 yards rushing and 75 yards passing.

Beyond the victory, Bowden was happy that his players had played their second game in a row without making any critical mental mistakes.

The victory gave them their fourth conference win and set the stage for their biggest contest of the season against the Gordon Military Cadets.

South Georgia Tigers vs Gordon Military Cadets

THE GORDON MILITARY CADETS, who unexpectedly defeated the Tigers in their season opener, would be coming to the game with a perfect conference record. The Tigers, whose conference record stood at 4 wins and one loss, knew they had to win if they wanted to share the conference title with Gordon and reconcile their earlier loss.

Nothing short of defeating the seemingly unconquerable Gordon eleven would make their season a success and put the embarrassment of their first game behind them. The excuses they'd used all season to justify their loss at the season opener wouldn't be worth spit if they lost again.

This time, the matchup was going to be played on the Tigers' home field. It had been advertised as the main event of South Georgia's homecoming week, and Bowden was hoping that a partisan crowd would give his players the extra incentive they needed to win.

As anticipated, on Saturday, November 17, the stands at South Georgia's College Field were packed with spirited alumni.

As the game got underway, the Cadets received the opening kickoff and quickly moved the football from their 22-yard line to the 35, picking up a quick first down. South Georgia fans were tense in the stands, fearing the Cadets had already taken the game's momentum away from the Tigers.

Stumpy Franklin, however, had something else in mind. On the Cadets' next play, he broke through the line of scrimmage and introduced their fullback to the real brand of Tiger football. His bell-ringing tackle not only knocked their runner backward, it caused the football to fly out of his hands as well. When it hit the ground, Homer Sowell was there to fall on it at the Cadets' 31-yard line.

The South Georgia Tigers were ready for revenge. On their first play from scrimmage, Bobby Dixon got them rolling by plowing through the Cadets' defense for 17 yards. Everett Graham and Larry DeLoach combined their efforts and moved it 9 more yards to the 8-yard line. Once they reached the 8-yard line, Wilkinson rolled out behind a wall of blockers and they ran in tandem into the end zone for the first touchdown of the game. Homer Sowell bisected the goal posts, and South Georgia took a very quick 7-0 lead over a stunned Gordon squad.

Control of the game seemed to shift to the Cadets' after they stripped the ball from a Tiger running back. That is until Stumpy Franklin, who apparently had decided to make this game personal, charged into their backfield and sacked the quarterback for a 12-yard loss.

After that South Georgia disabled the Cadets' running game, forcing them to resort to a fourth down pass that fell incomplete in the end zone.

Once the Tigers regained possession of the football, DeLoach, Graham, and Pichelmayer started a long, slow, but productive drive to the Cadets' goal line.

At the 29-yard line, Wilkinson rifled a quick pass to Homer Sowell for 13 more yards. On their next play, Bobby Pate picked up 14 more, racing to the 2-yard line. Spencer Goad brought the drive to its conclusion when he charged into the end zone. The first period ended shortly afterward with the Tigers leading the Cadets 13-0.

Early in the second quarter, the Tigers lead was cut to 7 points when GMC scored their own 6-pointer, momentarily reenergizing the Cadets—until Pate returned their kickoff 55 yards to their 35-yard line and extinguished their short-lived enthusiasm. After Pate's return, Goad ripped off 29 yards and moved the football to the Cadets' 6-yard line. Once the ball was lined up on the 6, Wilkinson called on Goad again, and this time he couldn't be stopped. He stepped into the end zone for the Tigers' third touchdown.

In the third quarter, the game turned back into a standoff until Jerry Holland snapped the deadlock by intercepting a Cadet pass. Two plays later, Fred Levy and Rosby Mulkey opened a huge hole in the Cadets' defensive line, and Goad took off on a 41-yard jaunt for another Tiger score.

After the Tigers' scored their fourth touchdown, the Cadets initiated their best offensive drive of the game, moving the football from their own 25-yard line across the Tigers' 30.

By the time they got inside the Tigers' 30-yard line, the game clock was already ticking off the last few minutes of the contest, so in desperation, their quarterback attempted a down-and-out pass to their tight end. But Pichelmayer intercepted the pass, ran it back 50 yards to the Cadets' 20-yard line, and put an end to any threat the Cadets may have posed.

Even though the game was out of the Cadets' reach, the Tigers didn't slow down. Two plays later, Goad, who had been the Cadets' biggest tormentor all night, leaped into the end zone from 4 yards out for another TD.

The fifth touchdown gave the Tigers an impressive 33-6 victory.

The win also meant South Georgia had captured a share of the Georgia State Junior College Conference Championship, and it validated what every player on the Tigers' team had felt all season: they shouldn't have lost their first game to the Cadets.

In conference play, both teams finished the season with five wins and one loss. In this particular game, the Tigers' offense outrushed the Cadets' 225 yards to 85 and dominated most of the game.

Coaches Bowden and Gibson couldn't have been happier with their team's performance. Gibson was especially proud of the linemen saying, "Our boys were ready and determined tonight, and it would be hard for me to single out any one particular lineman above another—they all looked good, even Gulbrandsen, who played injured most of the game."

It wasn't hard for anyone to single out Spencer Goad. The big fullback gained more than 100 yards rushing, scored 4 touchdowns, and averaged more than 10 yards per carry.

Every Tiger was proud of the win, but Bull Smith probably said it best when he stated, "This was one game we came to win, and nothing or nobody was going to keep us from doing that." The Tigers' attitude allowed them to dominate a game that many sportswriters had already written off for them by predicting that Gordon would win it and the conference championship.

The last thing people heard Bowden say as he walked off the field was, "This was one game where our boys played up to everyone's preseason expectations."

At the conclusion of the 1956 season, Roger Wilkinson, who missed most of the first part of the season with a back injury, and Rosby Mulkey, who played injured a good part of the season, were both selected as members of the National Junior College All-American team, and as first team members of the Georgia State Junior College Conference All-State team. This was the second year in a row that South Georgia had two players selected to the All-American team.

In addition to Wilkinson and Mulkey, Stumpy Franklin, Jerry Holland, and Homer Sowell were selected as members of the conference's All-State first team. South Georgia placed more players on the All-American team and All-State team than any other school in their conference, which was a high honor for both Bowden and Gibson.

14

LOOKING BACK TO LESSONS LEARNED

After defeating the Gordon Cadets in their final conference game and earning a well-deserved share of the Georgia Junior College Conference Championship, the South Georgia Tigers had just about completed their season—except for a non-conference game, scheduled on Thanksgiving Day, against Florida State University's freshman team.

The Tigers were pretty cavalier about the game, not just because they'd already won a part of their own conference's championship, but because playing the Seminoles' freshman team in the last game of the year was like playing a poker game with the deck stacked against you.

To fully understand the ridiculousness of the game, one would have to understand more about collegiate football in the 1950s. In that era, the National Collegiate Athletic Association (NCAA), the governing body of all Division I college athletic rules, of which FSU was a member but South Georgia wasn't, prohibited freshman football players from playing on varsity teams.

As a result, members of the NCAA had freshman teams made up "primarily" of freshman athletes. "Primarily" being the key word here, because toward the end of any season, the teams would more than likely have freshmen, sophomores, juniors, and sometimes even seniors playing on freshman teams—which were later called "B Teams."

This situation was unique to the period, and it gave those upper classmen who were good enough to make their school's varsity team but, for a variety of reasons, hadn't gotten a lot of playing time during the season an excellent opportunity to gain some valuable game experience playing on their freshmen team.

The game between the FSU freshmen and the South Georgia Tigers, scheduled at the end of both teams' seasons, gave Florida State the perfect opportunity to move any number of second- and third-team varsity players to their so-called freshman team to get more game experience. The Tigers chances of getting a fair shake were almost none.

Knowing that FSU's freshman team would be loaded with great players and would probably outnumber South Georgia's players by at least two to one, the Tigers could do nothing but look forward to playing another game and meeting another challenge.

South Georgia Tigers vs Florida State Freshman Seminoles

On THANKSGIVING DAY, November 22, 1956, the Florida State Freshman Seminoles showed up at South Georgia's College Field with approximately sixty players suited up and ready to do battle with the Tigers. The number seemed excessive for a freshman team, but it wasn't surprising to anyone at South Georgia. It was, however, imposing, especially when compared to the Tigers' much smaller roster of thirty-six players.

The game got underway on a bright, sunny fall day at 2 p.m. when FSU kicked off to the Tigers. The Tigers started the game with the same intensity they had played with in their last three conference games, seemingly undaunted by FSU. Not only were they undaunted, the Tiger linemen clearly dominated the line of scrimmage. Tiger running backs were able to pick up several productive gains and move the football closer to the Seminoles' goal line on every play. After reaching the 8-yard line, Everett Graham raced around his left-end and into the end zone, scoring the first touchdown of the contest. Homer Sowell added the extra point, and the Tigers took a surprising 7-0 lead early in the first quarter.

For the remainder of the first quarter, the Tigers' determination kept the Seminoles offense scoreless. Conversely, they were able to add 3 more points to their score when Sowell kicked his first and only field goal of the year, giving the seemingly fearless Tigers a 10-0 lead at the end of the first quarter, and made it appear they were controlling the game.

The Tigers looked good until midway through the second quarter when the FSU coaches started shuffling fresh players into the game.

The fresh players had an immediate impact on the tiring Tigers, and the Seminoles scored their first touchdown and extra point, reducing the Tigers' lead to 3 points.

Once the game's momentum shifted to the Seminoles, it was easy for FSU to score another touchdown, convert the extra point, and take a 14-10 lead just before halftime.

In the second half, the Tigers came back reenergized and played on even footing with the Seminoles through most of the third quarter—scoring tit-for-tat touchdowns, making the score 21-17 in favor of the Seminoles.

By the end of the third quarter, the Tigers were still taking the fight to the Seminoles, repeatedly pushing them back into their end of the field and threatening to score again while the Seminoles struggled to hold on to their 4-point lead.

Once the final quarter started, though, the weary Tigers were feeling the strain of being on the field so long without a break. The Seminoles, on the other hand, had plenty of fresh players, and once they started rotating them onto the field, they were able to keep the Tigers away from their goal line. The Seminoles managed to score one more touchdown, making the final score 27–17.

The Tigers' loss gave them a 5–4 season record—a record no one would have believed before the season began. Most blamed it on the injuries the Tigers' suffered, but Bowden had other thoughts. "We lost because the other team played better than we did," he'd say. Or he'd say, "We lost because I didn't call the right play at a critical time." Sometimes he said the other team was better prepared or better coached, but he always took most of the blame himself.

His explanations, whatever they were, go back to the leadership philosophy he's relied on since the beginning of his coaching career. In its most basic form, he believes that the head coach is always responsible for what happens to his team. He may have changed in many ways since his first years at South Georgia to accommodate the changing times, but this aspect of his personality has remained firm. His philosophy of what a head football coach should be and what his responsibilities are hasn't deviated much since those first years. If anything, it has only matured and grown stronger.

It's well known that Bowden loves the game of football and loves to win, but he has never compromised his first commitment: to build honorable characteristics and high moral standards in his players. His calling has always been higher than being the winningest football coach in the history of the game, and he believes that his success has been a gift from God. Therefore, he believes he must use his gift to be a positive influence whenever and wherever possible.

Today, he's frequently asked to speak to young, aspiring football players about the game and life in general. He frequently starts his speeches by telling his audience that he has a very distinct advantage over them in what he believes is right and wrong and what he's about to say, because he has been where they are, and he has been where many of them want to go.

He then tells them that if they want to be successful in anything, including football, it is his firm belief that they need to set some very important priorities for how they live.

According to Bowden, the priorities are as follows: God, family, country, and goals. Priority number one is to seek God's will. Priority number two is to love and respect parents and siblings, and to help them in a time of need. Priority three is to be a good student in order to be a good citizen. Finally, priority four, especially as it relates to football, is to set goals, dedicate time and energy to achieving the goals, and respect teammates, coaches, and opponents.

It may sound simple, but it took years of studying God's Word, being an inquisitive student of human nature, and being involved with the game of football for Bowden to find his mantra. And the 1956 football season at South Georgia was one of the most important years of study for him. It was his second year as a head football coach, and, with few exceptions, he had been bombarded and sometimes overwhelmed by new experiences, new challenges, and even a few surprises.

Of course, the bombardment shaped his coaching and leadership philosophies and influenced his coaching career more than any other period in his life.

He continued learning, even after the football season was over, when he had a chance to look back and examine what had occurred.

One thing he realized very quickly was that a team's success didn't always rest on physical attributes. In the past, he had been taught to believe that a player's athletic skill, his size, and maybe his speed were the most important characteristics to look at when considering a player's potential. Few if any mental attributes, beyond making sure that every player was academically eligible, were considered. But after a season riddled with reoccurring mental mistakes, he decided not to place so much emphasis on the physical.

He also learned that a player's attitude, his willingness to work together with other team members, and his ability to control his emotions during a game were just as important as other factors he had used as his guide.

Another area he began to think more about was size. Most coaches thought the biggest player was always the best, and prior to the 1956 season, Bowden had been inclined to agree. But, as the season progressed, he began to think about whether a larger player could play for a prolonged period of time and still maintain his superiority. The question of stamina was important in the '50s. Most players, especially linemen, were generally on the field for the entire game. A player who weighed 250-plus pounds would be carrying that weight around for an extended period of time in a physically stressful environment, which meant the big players were usually exhausted before the end of the second quarter. By the time the final buzzer sounded, the big guys were just trying to stay vertical on the field.

Bowden and Gibson realized this phenomenon early in the season. After the first game, they replaced the largest player on the team, who weighed about 276 pounds, with one that was about forty pounds lighter. Rosby Mulkey, the lighter player, started every game for the rest of the season.

Three weeks after starting Mulkey, another example of bigger not always being better played out. Two players were competing for the starting center position. The player first selected to be on the starting team weighed approximately 260 pounds and was an outstanding athlete, but because of his size, he had to push himself and his body to extremes during a game. During the latter minutes of the Tigers' fourth game, when he was playing on nothing but willpower, he slipped and seriously injured his ankle. His injury was serious enough that he missed the last five games of the season. Of course, anyone can argue that the likelihood of his getting injured was high under any circumstances, but in reality, because he had pushed himself past exhaustion, the likelihood of his injury wasn't just a probability—it was almost a sure thing.

His replacement, Jerry Holland, who weighed at least sixty pounds less, finished the season as the Tigers' starting center and, after the season was over, was selected as a member of the Georgia State Junior College Conference All-State first team.

The 1956 season was special. Bowden learned and refined some of the most pivotal basics of his philosophy that season, and the players from that year have never forgotten his leadership.

Coach Bobby Bowden 1956

Early photograph of the South Georgia College campus

1955

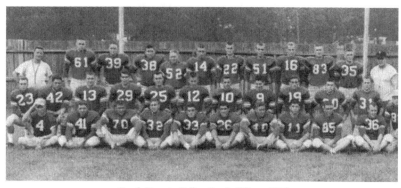

South Georgia College Football Team 1955
Row 3 L to R: Coach Bowden, R. Johnson, H. Smith, J. Kicklighter, B. Wilson, L. Studdard,
M. Ayers, M. Roberts, J. Barber, H. Sowell, B. Sowell, Asst. Coach Mvros
Row 2 L to R: V. Brinson, C. Gulbrandsen, L. Smith, B. Childs, B. Hayes, R. Wilkinson, R. Kelley,
B. Thornton, B. Dixon, J. DePalma, E. Graham
Row 1 L to R: J. Yeomans manager, M. Cooper, R. Mulkey, M. Adams, B. Franklin, B. Keys, J. Parker,
F. Levy, C. Morris, R. South, D. Suttles manager

Coach Bobby Bowden & Asst. Coach Sam Mvros 1955

Football players enjoying a picnic on campus 1955

1956

South Georgia College Football Team 1956

Row 3 L to R: M. Guthrie, T. Logue Manager, L. Studdard, J. Pichelmeyer, C. Gulbrandsen, W. Lavender, J. Holland, J. Barber, B. Sowell, B. Pate, R. Johnson, F. Miles, R. Mulkey, A. Johnson, L. Wood, M. Ayers, G. Hersey, Coach B. Bowden

Row 2 L to R: R. Hobbs, L. Duncan, D. Snipes, B. Schofill, R. Minchew, H. Sowell, D. Hall, D. Garrett, F. Levy, B. Dixon, S. Goad, E. Mixon, V. Brinson, B. Nauright, Coach V. Gibson

Row 1 L to R: P. Armstrong Manager, R. Wilkinson, L. Smith, T. Boney, L. DeLoach, D. Elder, E. Graham, B. Franklin, V. Giles, W. Vickers, J. Bowen, B. Barwick

Homer Sowell #25 advancing the football against Gordon Military College 1956

Jimmy Bowen running against Florida State University's freshman team on Thanksgiving Day 1956—Dewayne Elder #10 and Ed Mixon (on the ground) cleared the way for Bowen

Spencer Goad scoring a touchdown against Gordon Military College

Everett Graham #17 and Rosby Mulkey #23 leading the way for Bobby Pate against Georgia Military College—Jerry Holland #38 in the background

1956 Football team get on the "Blue Goose" to travel to an away game
L to R: Malcolm Ayers, Rosby Mulkey, Cecil Morris, Bobby Pate, Ronald Minchew, Leeon
"Bull" Smith, Lynford Wood, Everett Graham, Douglas Garrett
On the bus L to R: Spencer Goad, Tommy Johns (manager), unknown, and Bill Schofill

Coach Bowden on campus 1956

Football players relax on campus 1956
Back row L to R: Bobby Pate, Leeon "Bull" Smith, Homer "Old
Dad" Sowell, Bobby Dixon, Win Lavender
Front row: Jimmy Bowen

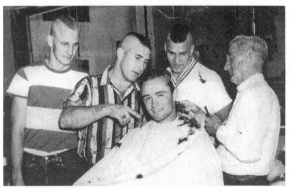

Players give barber instructions on how to cut Vernon "Pee Wee"
Brinson's Mohawk haircut 1956
Players L to R: Jerome "Blinkey" Barber, Mitchell "Ape" Adams,
Leeon "Bull" Smith

Coach Bobby Bowden and Coach Vince Gibson 1956

1957

Bobby Pate scoring another Tiger touchdown 1957

Coach Bobby Bowden and players 1957
Front row L to R: Weyman Vickers, Ed Mixon, and John Robert O'Neal
Back row L to R: Joe Wallis, Fred Dollar, Coach Bowden, Bobby Pate,
and Jim King

Coach Vince Gibson and players 1957
Front row L to R: Tommy Boney and Dewayne Elder.
Back row L to R: Hugh Gibbs, Ronald Minchew, Coach Gibson,
DeWitt Galloway, and Min Skoofalos

*Verlyn Giles scoring the Tigers' first touchdown against
Presbyterian College B team 1957*

1958

South Georgia College Football Team 1958
*Jimmy Thompson, Herbert Miller, David Parrish, Jim Alvarez, Min Skoofalos, George Faircloth, Bill
Lesky, Preston Nix, Richard Finley, Turk Gibbs, David Hughes, Ray Parker, Sam Smith, Bonwell Royal,
Bob Jones, Jimmy Norton, Harold Crews, Wayne Jackson, Don Sellers, Harry Brown, Hueland Hill,
B.B. Braddock, James Jacobelli, Fred Dollar, Billy Benton, John Porterfield, Tony Bell, George Versprille,
Robert Lairsey, Bobby Jackson, Joe Sears, Bill Black, Larry Gaylor, Carl Shepherd
(names not in order)*

Members of the alumni team during homecoming in 1958

2006

Bobby and Ann Bowden leading the food line at the 2006 Bobby Bowden Reunion at South Georgia College

Coach Bowden at the 2006 Reunion

15

BOWDEN DREAMS OF A
LESS STRESSFUL YEAR

Shortly after the 1956 season came to a close, Bowden started thinking about the next season and hoping it would be a lot less stressful than his first two years at South Georgia.

While he knew that being a head football coach would always be demanding and often stressful, he expected the experience he gained during the previous two years to make his third year a little more comfortable, if not less demanding. In many ways, he thought, he had already had his feet to the fire.

He was looking forward to concentrating more on football now that he wasn't coaching basketball and wouldn't be distracted as much by his other duties and responsibilities. In the past, it seemed like he was always playing catch-up just to stay on top of his day-to-day activities and keep from being drowned in his numerous other duties.

But then he came crashing back to reality and realized that he still had to get through another spring training, coach another baseball season, and work another summer of around-the-clock second and third jobs.

The thought of another summer filled with additional jobs certainly wasn't something he was looking forward to, but spring training and putting together a new football team was. Spring training was a time when he could get away from many of his other obligations and just think about football. It would give him and Coach Gibson a glimpse of what kind of talent they could expect in the next season, as well as an opportunity to reevaluate some of the players they expected to be returning from the 1956 team.

Bowden and Gibson were especially looking forward to seeing what Blinkey Barber, John Robert O'Neal, Buzzy Nauright, and Al Johnson could do. All four were red-shirted in 1956 because of injuries, but were now healthy and ready to start spring training.

Hoping for another winning season, Bowden and Gibson were eager to see how much Bobby Pate, Chico Elder, Tommy Boney, Ed Mixon, Bill Schofill, Doug Garrett, and Weyman Vickers had improved with a year of experience under their belts. Most of them had played backup roles in 1956, but they had all proved their worth to the team.

The coaches also expected a whole new crop of players. Some, already students at SGC, had expressed interest in participating in spring training and joining the team.

It wasn't long after spring training got underway before Bowden and Gibson decided that this group would be more than able to stand on its own merits. Past successes of the 1955 and 1956 teams were history, and 1957 was going to be a new beginning for the Tigers. Even with a contingent of twelve players returning from the 1956 team, every starting position was up for grabs.

Not only did the new group boast athletic abilities, they were full of personality too. Several quickly became known for their exploits off the field as well as on.

One of the players who fell into this mold was a big lineman whose genealogy dated back to the Cherokee tribes in North Carolina. Because of his heritage, he was quickly tagged with the nickname "Chief."

Chief was probably the oldest and biggest player on the team, and he wasn't timid about using his age and size to intimidate his teammates of lesser stature and experience. He was about twenty-six or twenty-seven years old—as old as, or older than, both Bowden and Gibson—and he towered over everyone, standing about 6'5" in his bare feet and easily tipping the scales at 250 pounds. Even weighing that much, his body mass index was only in the single digits—he was built like Hercules.

Chief's most unique quality, beyond his size and prowess on the football field, was his propensity for finding trouble. Sometimes he went looking for it, but other times, even if he had his eyes closed, it found him.

This was especially true when he partook of any alcohol, which he occasionally delighted in when he could afford it.

When Chief first came to South Georgia, he told Bowden that he was a military veteran and that he had played football the previous year at Florida State University. Because communications were not what they are today, no one bothered to verify his claims. If they had, they would have discovered that Chief conveniently omitted that he had left the military and FSU under less than favorable circumstances.

During spring training, Chief began to take an interest in some of the attractive coeds at South Georgia, which wasn't unusual. But, to his dismay, he wasn't getting the response he desired—his admiration wasn't being reciprocated as he had hoped.

Part of the problem was baseball. A minor league team (part of the Georgia-Florida Class D Baseball League) was having its own training camp in town, and it seemed the South Georgia ladies had also caught the baseball players' eyes.

Being the keen person he was, Chief noticed that several of the young ladies he was attracted to seemed to be more interested in baseball players than him. He was so upset he started looking for an opportunity to challenge his competitors' manliness, and he didn't try to keep his intentions a secret.

After openly challenging the team and getting no takers, he decided to concoct his own story.

In his story, he was confronted by several players from the baseball camp and forced into a fight. He even went so far as to prepare a bandage, tape it to his face, and wear it to the dining hall one evening where he hoped he would be questioned by some of the coeds.

As luck would have it, that's exactly what happened, and Chief took great pleasure in reciting his imaginary story while explaining that his involvement was mainly in defense of the honor of certain young ladies. After reciting his story several times, he returned to his dormitory convinced that he would get the attention he wanted.

When he got back to the dorm, he told some of the other football players, including Stumpy Franklin and Bill Schofill, what he had done. Stumpy and Schofill, being inquisitive types, asked Chief what he was going to say when the bandage was removed and there wasn't a scratch on him. Chief, who hadn't bothered to plan beyond the present, couldn't come up with a believable answer. Stumpy suggested that the story would be much more credible if Chief would let him make a couple shallow cuts on his face so he would have a scar.

Stumpy probably wasn't serious, but Chief assumed he was, so he gave Stumpy permission to try his skills at re-sculpturing his face.

Once he had Chief's permission, Stumpy took a straight razor and went to work like a skilled surgeon making a short, shallow cut down one side of Chief's face. As soon as the blade touched Chief's face, he let out a cry loud enough to pierce the ears of everyone on campus; therefore, Stumpy and Schofill agreed, and Chief concurred, that one scar was probably sufficient.

Before they separated, however, Stumpy told Chief that if he could find a needle and thread, he could put a couple of sutures in his cheek, which Stumpy thought would really help his story. Fortunately for Chief, Stumpy wasn't able to find the equipment he needed, so they gave up on the idea of the sutures.

When Bowden noticed Chief's "injury," he didn't ask about it. This was one of the few times he figured he was better off not knowing.

It might have been a show of fortitude for Chief to allow Stumpy to take a blade to his face, but Chief wasn't the only tough player at spring training. Schofill proved his grit more than a few times.

Schofill came to South Georgia from Fort Valley, a small town in central Georgia known in the 1950s mainly for the Blue Bird bus manufacturing plant that employed the majority of residents of the town. Since there wasn't much else to talk about when a person thought of Fort Valley, Schofill made it his mission while at South Georgia to talk as often as he could about the bus manufacturing plant. He talked about it so much that some of his teammates started to think he was a personal envoy for the company, or at least had a financial interest in it.

His verbosity on the subject of the company, always delivered in a slow, deep monotone, and the fact that he weighed about 240 pounds, helped some of the younger players conceive the nickname "King-of-the-Board" Schofill. His larger-than-life persona also intimidated many of the younger players, which he obviously enjoyed. Sometimes he'd initiate an incident to prove his caliber, and other times, fate would intercede on his behalf and help him in his endeavor.

One particular incident that boosted Schofill's reputation happened on the field during a blocking drill. Schofill, who didn't wear a face guard, got hit in the face and his nose split wide open. This wasn't just a bloody nose. The fissure ran all the way down the middle of his nose and blood gushed out and down his face in such volume that it looked like a transfusion might be necessary.

Schofill ripped off his helmet, stood straight up, and stared downfield with glazed eyes, all the while snorting and spitting blood like a dying bull.

Since there weren't any medically trained personnel at the practice field or on campus, Gibson told Tiny Logue, one of the team managers, to drive Schofill to "Doc Johnson's" office in Douglas. With those instructions, Tiny handed Schofill a dirty wet towel to hold on his nose, and they were off to the doctor's office.

At Dr. Johnson's office, Schofill was making a big bloody mess in the waiting room and then in the examination room. He was mad about getting hurt, which was obvious to Johnson when he asked Schofill about his nose and he wouldn't admit he was in pain.

Sensing that Schofill wanted to act tough, Johnson responded by not showing him a lot of sympathy when he cleaned his nose. He even sewed it up without any sedative. Schofill admitted later that he almost fainted, but that didn't stop Johnson.

After Johnson finished repairing Schofill's nose, he released him without any further instructions other than to tell him that if his face got to hurting too much he could take a couple of aspirins and lie down for a few minutes.

By then Schofill's face had swollen so much he was almost unrecognizable.

On the way back to the campus, the pain and swelling seemed to be getting worse, so Schofill thought he should probably go straight to the dormitory and lie down for the remainder of the afternoon. But he had his reputation to consider, so he decided to return to practice so none of his teammates would think he'd gone soft. He had worked too hard building his reputation to let this destroy it.

Surely, he thought, when Coach Gibson saw his face, he would insist that he sit out for the remainder of that day's practice, but he quickly learned that assumptions are usually incorrect when dealing with football coaches.

When they got back to the field and he walked up to Gibson, Gibson grabbed his jersey and shook him, announcing, "Look at this man; here's a real football player with the right attitude. He's not going to let a little bloody nose keep him from practicing." With that, Gibson gave him a slap on the butt and told him to get on the field.

"Somehow I survived the rest of that practice without any further damage to my nose," Schofill said, "but the next thirty minutes were probably the longest thirty minutes of my life." His reputation wasn't tarnished though.

Schofill couldn't out-tough Chief though, who sometimes went too far and actually ended up damaging his reputation, instead of protecting it. One Saturday morning, near the end of spring training, Bowden got a phone call from the Coffee County sheriff's office.

According to the sheriff, he had one of South Georgia's football players in jail, and since he was a big supporter of South Georgia College and its football team, he wanted to work with Bowden to resolve the player's problem without any legal action—that is if Bowden would take responsibility for the player.

It seemed that the player in question was Chief and he had gotten into a bit of trouble the night before at a local veteran's club after a few too many beers. The sheriff told Bowden that Chief had gotten into an argument with the club manager, and when the sheriff's deputies couldn't calm him down, they had to arrest him.

After Chief was locked up in the holding tank for intoxicated prisoners, he set fire to the mattress in the cell and tried to burn the jail down while he was still in it.

After a lengthy discussion with the sheriff, Bowden agreed to discipline Chief when he got back to the campus if the sheriff would release him.

Later, Bowden had a long talk with Chief and explained to him that what he had done was wrong, and that it had embarrassed him, the school, and the entire football team. He also told Chief that, as punishment, he would have to do some extra work at practice. Chief accepted this punishment without any argument and, according to Bowden, appeared to be sincerely sorry for what had happened.

Bowden concluded his admonishment by saying, "If you have to drink in the future, you need to go someplace away from Douglas and out of Coffee County." When he said this, Bowden wasn't trying to encourage him to continue drinking; what he was trying to do was emphasize that he expected Chief to be a good role model in the local community. He also assumed Chief understood what he was saying.

Unfortunately, Bowden lived to regret his assumption. A couple weeks later, he received a call from another sheriff. This time it was from the Irwin County sheriff. The Irwin County sheriff informed Bowden that he had Chief in jail in Ocilla because he had been involved in a fight at a bar the night before.

The sheriff also explained to Bowden that Chief was probably facing some very serious charges because when his deputies tried to break up the fight, Chief refused to comply with their instructions and they had to use seven deputies to subdue and arrest him. According to the sheriff, after Chief got some sleep and sobered up, he asked the sheriff to call Coach Bowden.

Bowden and the Sheriff eventually worked out an arrangement so that Chief could be released to his custody.

For the remainder of that spring quarter, through the summer months, and into the fall and the start of the new football season, Bowden went out of his way to help Chief stay out of trouble—even arranging for him to get a football scholarship during the summer quarter so he could stay in school and make up some much needed academic courses.

During this same period, Bowden frequently talked to Chief and tried to encourage him to use his talents as an athlete to make something of his life.

According to several players, after the summer was over and the 1957 season started, Chief seemed to be a completely different person, committed to changing his life and doing whatever Bowden asked him to do.

Bowden was happy with Chief's new commitment and sincerely hoped that the worst was behind them. At the same time, he had to laugh at himself for ever thinking that 1957 might be less stressful than the previous two years.

16

THE 1957 SEASON GETS STARTED

*S*outh Georgia's 1957 fall football camp started on September 9, and on the first day, sixty-five candidates showed up. Most were newcomers, except for about two dozen who had already joined the team during spring training and twelve or thirteen who were returning lettermen from the 1956 season. Of the returning lettermen, only one had been a starter, which meant every position was wide open. The opportunity intensified the fierce competition of the first two weeks.

Anyone who knows anything about playing football understands that the first two or three weeks of practice generally separate the men from the boys, and Bowden and Gibson knew this well. The "men," those who didn't quit and turn in their uniforms, would eventually make up the 1957 Tigers football team. The starting team was usually identifiable within the first two weeks as well. If there were some positions still in question, it was due to heated competition.

For example, at the end of the first two weeks, Bowden still hadn't decided on the starting quarterback. It was still a toss-up between returning letterman Chico Elder and newcomer Ted Moseley, who was one of the biggest surprises of preseason camp. Most observers were confident that Elder would eventually get the nod, especially since he had done a commendable job replacing All-American Roger Wilkinson the previous year, but Bowden apparently hadn't seen the need to rush his decision.

There was also a battle shaping up for the starting fullback position.

Fred Dollar was a star on the track team in 1956, winning the 100- and 200-yard dashes at the Georgia State Intercollegiate Junior College track meet in Macon. Bill Black, a newcomer, was completely undeterred by Dollar's speed. He was one of the hardest working players on the team, and he had made it clear to Bowden and Dollar that he had no intention of spending a lot of time sitting on the sidelines. With that attitude, Dollar was assured that he would never be able to relax, because Black would always be breathing down his neck trying to unseat him.

Bobby Pate, the only starter returning from 1956 team, captured the starting left halfback slot ahead of Doug Garrett, but the right halfback position was still a dogfight between John Robert O'Neal, Weyman Vickers, and Buzzy Nauright. All three were outstanding running backs who had already proven themselves in 1956 and spring training. Add Robert Lairsey, a hard-running newcomer, to the mix and it was easy to see that the final selection would be difficult to make. In fact, Bowden didn't name a starter at this position until just before their first game.

Ronald Minchew jumped in front of Wayne Walker for the center position. Tommy Boney and Ed "Mr. IQ" Mixon, back from the year before, were firmly fixed in starting guard positions, and Richard Gamble and Gaylon Rush, two newcomers, were listed as backups.

Before the start of the season, Gibson had penciled in Al Johnson as a probable starter at one of the guard positions, but during the first week of practice, he reinjured the arm that had been a problem for him the year before, and this time the injury required surgery. The surgery was expected to make it impossible for him to play again this season.

Bill Schofill had little trouble recapturing the right-tackle slot, while several other hopefuls were still battling it out for the left side position. Those still in contention for the starting left tackle slot were Joe Wallis, Hugh Gibbs, and Chief. It was no secret that Chief would probably get the starting call if he stayed out of trouble, but the coaches apparently wanted to wait until right before the first game to announce their selection.

The flanker positions were loaded with as much talent as any position. Blinkey Barber, a fullback in 1955 and in 1956 before he was red shirted, and James "Min" Skoofalos, a newcomer, were the front-runners for the starting roles at the end positions. There were several others though who wouldn't give up their hopes of knocking either Barber or Skoofalos from his perch and taking over one of the two end positions before the season started. Most notable in this group were Jim Alvarez, Jim King, Tillman Norris, and Don Sellers.

The Tigers' first game of the 1957 season was scheduled to be played on a neutral field in LaGrange, Georgia, against the West Georgia Braves. As the opening date got closer, the entire team seemed as anxious to get the season going as any previous team under Bowden's leadership, but this team was healthier and had more players ready to play than any of his other teams in the past.

The following players made up the Tigers 1957 squad:

NAME	POSITION	WEIGHT	NUMBER
Ray Adams	Tackle	190	24
Jim Alvarez	End	180	15
Malcolm Ayers	End	178	32
Jerome "Blinkey" Barber	End	185	16
Bill Benton	Halfback	150	35
W.H. "Bill" Black	Fullback	183	19
Tommy Boney	Guard	175	28
B.B. Braddock	Quarterback	186	26
Fred Dollar	Fullback	185	11
DeWayne "Chico" Elder	Quarterback	165	10
DeWitt Galloway	Tackle	212	40
Richard Gamble	Guard	178	29
Doug Garrett	Halfback	180	22

Turk Gibbs	Tackle	210	20
Verlyn Giles	Halfback	155	99
George Hunt	Guard	185	83
George Hersey	Halfback	160	21
Jim King	End	212	39
Robert Lairsey	Halfback	190	34
Ronald Minchew	Center	193	33
Ed "Mr. IQ" Mixon	Guard	220	41
Phillip Moore	Fullback	186	36
Ted Moseley	Quarterback	175	30
Ralph "Buzzy" Nauright	Halfback	180	17
Tillman Norris	End	185	31
Jimmy Norton	Guard	165	37
John Robert O'Neal	Halfback	180	25
David Parrish	End	188	37
Bobby Pate	Halfback	165	18
Chief	Tackle	248	43
Gaylon Rush	Guard	210	45
Bill Schofill	Tackle	240	44
Joe Sears	Halfback	168	12
Don Sellers	End	195	27
Min Skoofalos	End	193	38
Wayne Walker	Center	180	23
Joe Wallis	Tackle	198	42
Weyman Vickers	Halfback	148	13

South Georgia Tigers vs West Georgia Braves

THE TIGERS OPENED THEIR 1957 SEASON on September 29 against the West Georgia Braves in a torrential rainstorm. Considering the field conditions, Bowden thought it would be to their advantage if they kicked off instead of receiving, even though they won the coin toss and could have received.

It turned out to be a wise decision, considering how much trouble the Braves' had trying to run with the football on the wet, slippery turf. After three tries, they were forced to punt from their 25-yard line, but the water-soaked ball only carried for a short distance before coming down at their 46.

The game quickly devolved into a mud-hole brawl, but that didn't stop the Tigers from taking control and a 6-point lead when Fred Dollar literally high stepped his way into pay dirt from 3 yards out for the game's first touchdown.

After their touchdown, Min Skoofalos kicked off for the Tigers, and his long, low boot sailed deep downfield hitting the ground inside the Braves' 15-yard line before skidding into the end zone. Once the ball slid across the goal line and rolled dead in the end zone the Braves seemed confused and ran away from it, which made it possible for Doug Garrett to jump on it for another Tiger score, giving the Tigers a very early 12-point lead.

When the Tigers kicked off to the Braves for the third time, lady luck looked down on the Braves more favorably, and they were able to score their first touchdown. To Bowden's chagrin, penalties against the Tigers were as much responsible for the Braves' score as anything else. The first quarter ended shortly thereafter with the Tigers still leading by 6 points.

The second quarter was more evenly matched. Both teams seemed to be having problems getting their offenses organized, which turned the quarter into a scoreless deep-water melee that was played primarily between the 20-yard lines.

In the third quarter, the Tigers finally got their offensive act together and scored two more touchdowns.

The first was set up when West Georgia's second-half kickoff barely made it to the 50-yard line before Blinkey Barber jumped on it.

The Tigers then put together their best offensive drive of the game. Bobby Pate started it off as he darted around his right end and ran to the Braves' 38-yard line. Then Elder hit John Robert O'Neal with a quick, flat pass, and O'Neal broke loose for another 31 yards. Once inside the Braves' 10-yard line, Dollar picked up 7 more yards before Elder brought the drive to a conclusion, jumping behind Bill Schofill and following him into the end zone. Elder kicked the extra point, and the Tigers took a 19-6 lead.

Shortly after the Tigers kicked off again, Dollar intercepted the Braves' first aerial attempt at their 25-yard line and returned it to the 16.

Buzzy Nauright took the ball and ran over several defenders before he was finally tripped up at the 4-yard line. Elder picked up another 2 yards, and then Dollar dove into the end zone, scoring the Tigers fourth and final TD of the game. Elder added the extra point, and the Tigers took home a well-deserved 26-6 victory in what some players still remember as the "Mud Bowl of 1957."

South Georgia held West Georgia's offense to a total of 84 yards rushing and zero yards through the air. The Tigers played an outstanding game, especially linemen Schofill, Barber, Mixon, and Boney, who were frequently in the Braves' backfield harassing the Braves' runners.

Normally, when a football team wins its first game of the season, it's a big confidence builder, which would have been true for the Tigers except that Bowden and Gibson still had vivid memories of their next opponent and their last game of the 1956 season.

Their opponent was none other than the Florida State University B team, and the game was scheduled to be played on their home field.

Neither Bowden nor Gibson could help but recall that it had only been a few short months since the very same team had come to South Georgia, showing up with more than sixty players. Their ability to keep a fresh team on the field for four quarters proved to be too much for the Tigers to overcome.

Their anxiety intensified when they learned that the FSU team was "loaded" with another group of outstanding players and had already defeated their first opponent by a very impressive 51-0 score. Bowden and Gibson had the seemingly impossible task of preparing their team to compete against an opponent that was capable of keeping a group of fresh, equally competent players on the field for an entire game.

South Georgia Tigers vs Florida State Seminoles B Team

ON SEPTEMBER 29, before either Bowden or Gibson was able to get comfortable with a strategy to beat them, the Tigers had to kick off to the Seminoles in Tallahassee.

To make the situation gloomier, the Seminoles ran their opening kickoff back 91 yards for a touchdown, converted the PAT, and took a 7-point lead before the game was fifteen seconds old.

Somehow, after that, Bowden and Gibson managed to pull the team together, and for the next thirty minutes they fought off an unrelenting ground and air attack and kept the score at 7-0 until the first half ended.

The struggle, however, took its toll. Several South Georgia players sustained injuries in the first half, including two key players whose injuries were so serious they wouldn't be able to play the second half. Several others would be playing at less than full speed due to minor injuries. In the locker room at half time, the entire starting team showed signs of weariness. It was obvious to Bowden and Gibson that all the injuries their players had sustained during the first half, plus signs that several of them were suffering from acute exhaustion, were definitely going to have a devastating effect on their play in the second half.

As expected, when they returned to the field for the second half, everything came crashing down at once. On the Tigers' first play from scrimmage after receiving the Seminoles' kickoff, the football was mishandled in the backfield and recovered by the Seminoles inside their 15-yard line. Because the Seminoles were primed and ready to pick up the tempo when the second half got underway, the fumble gave them just the jolt they needed.

Two plays later, they scored their second touchdown and the script was written for the rest of the contest.

Not only did the Seminoles dominate every aspect of the game, they capitalized on every mistake the Tigers made. To start with, the Tigers attempted to throw a short down-and-out pass, but the Seminoles grabbed it and ran it back for another TD.

The Seminoles kicked off again and this time the Tigers' offense got bogged down completely. When they tried to punt on fourth down, the Seminoles blocked the kick and turned it into another touchdown.

These three quick touchdowns not only added 20 more points to the Seminoles' score, they destroyed what little life the South Georgia players had left in them.

From that point until the final whistle, the Seminoles mauled the South Georgians, scoring two more touchdowns and a 24-yard field goal, which gave them a resounding 43-0 victory over the exhausted, dejected Tigers.

At no time were the Tigers ever a threat. Statistically, the Seminoles gained a combined total of 448 yards, rushing and passing, compared to the Tigers' 119 yards. The Tigers sealed their fate by turning the football over to the Seminoles five times in the second half—three times because of fumbles and twice because of thrown interceptions.

The defeat itself was bad enough for Bowden and his squad, but it paled in comparison to the problems he discovered once he started assessing the number of injured players that might not be able to play again for several days. Once he was fully aware of the damage the Seminoles' game had inflicted, he realized that this loss could hurt them for several weeks and possibly several games to come.

He was especially worried about their next game against the Middle Georgia Wolverines, which was scheduled for the next Thursday night instead of Saturday as usual. The Wolverines had always been a tough conference rival, and because of the Thursday game schedule, the Tigers would only have five days to recuperate, which meant that some of the injured players wouldn't be able to play, and this put them at a big disadvantage.

As Bowden and Gibson assessed the damage, they determined that at least two of their starters, Ed Mixon, a team captain, and John Robert O'Neal, would definitely not play. They selected Richard Gamble, a freshman guard, to replace Mixon, and Buzzy Nauright, a sophomore, to fill in for O'Neal at running back.

In addition to Mixon and O'Neal, five other starters suffered questionable wounds, and nobody knew for sure whether they would be able to play come game day. These players were: Blinkey Barber, Bobby Pate—the other team captain—Tommy Boney, Fred Dollar, and Chief.

Their injuries were less serious than Mixon's and O'Neal's, but they couldn't practice at full speed all week. With all the injuries, at least two-thirds of the starting lineup could be on the sideline when they kicked off to the Wolverines. Even with this initial dismal outlook, Bowden and Gibson were optimistic that every one of these players would at least be able to play some of the game, if not all of it.

South Georgia Tigers vs Middle Georgia Wolverines

On October 2, when the Tigers arrived in Cochran, the home of the Middle Georgia Wolverines, some of their injured players were still questionable, even though it was almost game time. Finally, just before their 8 p.m. kickoff, Bowden and Gibson decided that all of the regular starters would start the game, except Mixon and O'Neal.

Their decision was based primarily on what each player told the coaches, not on a medical examination or diagnosis. Once the game got underway, Bowden quickly noticed that some players were not playing up to their normal capabilities. Throughout the first quarter, the mediocrity of their play was only exceeded by their lack of enthusiasm. This was especially true on offense, but the Wolverines weren't doing much better.

After fifteen minutes of uninspired football, the first quarter ended with two big zeros on the scoreboard. The stalemate continued until the Wolverines broke the ice when they returned a Tiger punt 81 yards to score the first TD of the game in the late seconds of the second quarter. After adding the extra point, they went ahead of the Tigers by 7 points just before the end of the first half.

When the second half began, the Wolverines seemed more enthusiastic about the game than they were in the first half, but the Tigers were still unable to generate any energy or enthusiasm. Some fans thought the Wolverines were pumped up because they were ahead of a team that no other Wolverine team had beaten in over seventeen years.

Their excitement gave them the momentum they needed to pick up three successive first downs before fumbling the ball inside the Tigers' 10-yard line.

The fumble was the break the Tigers needed to turn the game around, but because they fumbled the ball back to the Wolverines before they were able to move it away from their goal line, it had the opposite effect.

When the Wolverines regained possession of the football, they were on the Tigers' 4-yard line, and they quickly scored their second touchdown. When they converted the point-after-touchdown, they increased their lead to 14 points.

For the rest of the third quarter and most of the fourth, the game was played in the middle of the field and neither team was able to add any more points to their score.

With five minutes remaining in the game, Bowden and Gibson substituted several reserve players into the contest.

The substitution might have been an act of desperation, or it might have been an opportunity to give the reserves some game experience, but for whatever reason, it stimulated the Tigers' offense, and they immediately initiated their best offensive drive of the game. It covered 67 yards and featured ball carrying by Phil Moore. Moore picked up 48 yards on five carries before he finally burst into the end zone from 5 yards out, giving the Tigers their only score. Chico Elder converted the PAT, making the score 14-7. A couple minutes later, the game ended and the Tigers had to accept being defeated by a team that had not beaten a South Georgia team in almost two decades.

This loss gave the Tigers a record of only one win against two defeats, which discouraged Bowden and Gibson. But more than anything else, they were discouraged and concerned by the way their team had played.

Being defeated by FSU's B team certainly wasn't anything to be happy about, but it could have been forgotten if they had bounced back and won their game against Middle Georgia. But since they didn't—they didn't even play like they wanted to win—Bowden and Gibson found themselves with more questions than answers. They wanted to know what had happened to their offensive game and their players' enthusiasm. Where was the drive and determination that this team had shown in their first game against West Georgia?

Bowden couldn't imagine how he had ever conceived the idea that 1957 was going to be less stressful than his first two years. But being the perpetual optimist that he was, he bounced back and decided to be thankful that the season was still young and that his team had a long week to recuperate and get ready for their next game. The season hadn't gone the way he had hoped, but he still felt confident his team could win if they were healthy.

The following Monday, the pressure to win was already starting to build. Practices were long and spirited, often becoming intense and emotional.

This intensity occasionally caused fights to erupt between players. Chief seemed more interested in fighting than anyone else, and on one occasion he even threatened Coach Gibson when Gibson stepped between him and another player to stop one of the fights.

Chief's threat disturbed Bowden, especially because he'd recently been told that Chief had threatened some of his teammates in the dormitory.

Bowden, as well as some of Chief's teammates, began to think

Chief was falling back into his old undisciplined ways. Some even questioned his mental state. Bowden knew he had to resolve the situation as soon as possible before it got out of hand.

The urgency of the situation eventually caused Bowden to do something he has regretted even to this day, more than fifty years later.

Back then Bowden had only himself to rely on when he had a problem to resolve or a difficult decision involving a player to make. After Chief tried to duke it out with Gibson at practice, Bowden started thinking about all the other problems he had caused.

The more he thought about it, the more he was convinced that his only recourse was to remove Chief from the team. Once he reached his decision, he knew he had to go to Chief's room and inform him. Bowden had no idea how Chief would react, so he decided he would just tell Chief that he had no other choice but to remove him from the team because he had threatened Coach Gibson. If necessary, he would emphasize that threatening a coach couldn't be excused.

He hoped Chief would accept the fact that threatening a coach was a serious enough violation and he wouldn't have to mention anything or anyone else. On his way to Chief's room, he thought about what he would say if it became necessary to calm Chief down. He decided that if it was necessary, he would tell Chief that he was willing to help him get on the football team at the University of Southern Mississippi in Hattiesburg, Mississippi, if he would learn to control his temper.

Bowden knew the coach at Southern Mississippi, and he thought that if Chief were receptive to the idea, he would have plenty of time to call the coach there and talk to him about Chief.

As is usually the case when a person fabricates a lie, especially a person unaccustomed to lying and who is under a lot of stress, the lie begins to grow and take on a life of its own. And this is exactly what happened when Bowden told Chief that he could no longer be a member of the team because he had threatened Coach Gibson.

Chief apologized and pleaded with Bowden to punish him some

other way; at one point he even suggested that Bowden use him as an example the next day at practice and punch him in the face in front of the other players. Bowden couldn't help but feel sorry for him, but he couldn't give in, so he continued to elaborate on his fabrication. When he did, his story got all twisted up, and he told Chief that he had already arranged for him to get a scholarship at Southern Mississippi if he could get to Hattiesburg right away and make their team.

Much to Bowden's surprise, Chief seemed excited about going to Southern Mississippi. Bowden was even more surprised when he heard a little while later that Chief had packed his suitcase, left campus, and was hitchhiking to Hattiesburg.

As soon as he found out, Bowden called the coach at Southern Mississippi to inform him that he had sent him an outstanding prospect, trying all the time to inflate Chief's abilities as a football player while downplaying his problem areas. After listening to Bowden's story, the Southern Mississippi coach told Bowden he was sorry, but he didn't have any more scholarships.

After Bowden realized he wasn't going to be able to convince the Southern Mississippi coach to let Chief join his team, he called the local sheriff and asked him to do anything he could to ensure that Chief didn't come back into Coffee County; just in case he decided to return to South Georgia.

Even today, Bowden says he is ashamed of the way he handled the situation with Chief. It was inexcusable. And it was one of the most difficult learning experiences of his life. First and foremost he regrets what he did because it was an offense against God when he lied. Secondly, he regrets it because he abandoned a player when he should have continued trying to help him. For these reasons, he admittedly had many sleepless nights after the incident. As a result, he promised himself that he would never lie to another player, no matter what the circumstances.

17

"DADGUMIT, HERE WE GO AGAIN!"

South Georgia Tigers vs Georgia Military Bulldogs

*B*owden was so puzzled by the loss to the Middle Georgia Wolverines and his players' lack of enthusiasm that he didn't really know what to expect when they took the field to play the Georgia Military Bulldogs on October 12. The only thing he did know for sure was that there was a dark cloud hanging over their heads, and their hopes for a successful season were already looking questionable. He also knew that they had to win this game if they expected to be in the running for another conference title.

For all these reasons, and probably many more, the Tigers' level of anxiety was at its peak as they looked forward to their game against the Bulldogs. When the day of the game finally arrived, adrenaline was pumping and butterflies were fluttering. Fortunately, after they received the kickoff and began executing their game plan, they settled down and got into a more relaxed rhythm. They even put together one of the most controlled drives of the season and were able to score the first touchdown of the game when Bobby Pate charged into the end zone from 27 yards out.

The touchdown soothed their nerves, boosted their enthusiasm, and strengthened their determination to win the game. With their rediscovered enthusiasm, it didn't take long for them to regain control of the football and start another beautiful march downfield.

The Tigers used a time-consuming running attack to get inside the Bulldogs' 10-yard line before time ran out in the first quarter. As soon as the second quarter got underway, John Robert O'Neal tore through the Bulldogs' secondary and shot across the last 9 yards to pay dirt. The 6-pointer gave the Tigers a solid 12-point lead while the game was still early in the second quarter.

After the Tigers kicked off to the Bulldogs for the third time, their defensive line, which included Bill Schofill, Hugh Gibbs, Tommy Boney, Ed Mixon, Min Skoofalos, and Blinkey Barber, dominated the line of scrimmage, and quickly forced the Bulldogs into another punting situation.

When the Tigers got the football back, Ted Moseley quickly got them moving with a sizzling 25-yard pass to Jim King. Afterward the Tigers went back to their running game, and Bobby Pate and Robert Lairsey ripped off two successive gains that covered another 43 yards.

From the 17-yard line, Lairsey tucked the pigskin under his arm, fell in behind Bill Schofill, and galloped across the goal line, scoring the Tigers' third touchdown. Moseley converted the extra point, and the Tigers went ahead of the Bulldogs by 19 points.

After scoring three unanswered touchdowns, some South Georgia players apparently got the idea they had the game won and could relax. Sensing their complacency, GMC picked up the pace and scored a touchdown just before the first half ended. Their touchdown trimmed the Tigers' lead to 13 points and gave the Bulldogs the game's momentum just before the first half ended.

Bowden was visibly upset. In the locker room, he pointed out that this game was a long way from over. He used expressions that have now become synonymous with his halftime pep talks, such as: "Now dadgumit boys, you can't just stop playing because you're 19 points ahead" or, "This is a sixty-minute game, and that means you've got to play hard-nosed football every play for sixty minutes. If any of you can't do that, I'll find you a nice seat on the sideline where you can watch someone else who will."

The players seemed to grasp the idea, so when they returned to the field, they were ready to rectify their first half mistakes and play with the same intensity and determination they had in the first quarter.

Led by Moseley, they took the second half kickoff and put together a drive that didn't stop until they crossed their opponent's
goal line. The offense was a well-oiled machine, mixing just the
right amount of running and passing plays until they reached the
Bulldogs' 6-yard line. Once they reached the 6, Fred Dollar brought
it to a conclusion when he raced across the goal line, scoring their
fourth touchdown.

After the Tigers scored their fourth TD, the Bulldogs tried desperately to compete with the Tigers, but their efforts were in vain
and they eventually had to punt the ball back to them.

Once the Tigers got the football again, they immediately initiated
another successful drive, covering 80 yards.

To get them moving, Moseley went to the air and connected with
Jim King for 16 yards. On the next play, Moseley faked another pass
before pitching the ball back to Bobby Pate who darted off-tackle for
another 15 yards to the Bulldogs' 49-yard line. Once the Tigers got
across the midfield marker, Fred Dollar took off on a 49-yard jaunt
through the Bulldogs' defense to score another 6-pointer. Jim King
converted the PAT, and the Tigers increased their lead to 25 points.

Even though the Tigers were leading by 25 points, they weren't
ready to slow down. After the fourth quarter got underway, Moseley
orchestrated what most modern-day football experts would describe
as a two-minute offensive drill, even though it was still very early in
the final quarter.

Dazzling the Bulldogs' defense with his passing accuracy, Moseley
completed two passes in quick succession to one of his favorite targets,
Jim King, for a combined 29 yards. He also connected with Pate on
a swing pass, and Pate stepped off another 12 yards. Finally, he hit
David Parrish in the end zone with a 14-yard pass for their sixth and
final touchdown. Jim King converted the extra point, and the Tigers
took home a well-earned 38-6 victory.

After the game, Bowden and Gibson singled out Tommy Boney,
Ted Moseley, and Fred Dollar for praise, saying that all three played

an outstanding game on both sides of the football.

The Tigers rushed for 317 yards and passed for 120, for a grand total of 437 yards. The Bulldogs could only manage 68 yards rushing and 87 yards through the air, for a total of 155 yards.

Both Bowden and Gibson thought their players had played their best game of the year, except that they racked up 145 yards in penalties. The penalties resurrected some 1956 nightmares, causing Bowden to exclaim, "Dadgumit, here we go again!"

But he brushed this worry aside, realizing his biggest worry was the fact that more than half of the starting lineup was still suffering with some sort of injury.

In fact, the most disconcerting thing about the GMC game was that some of his players, he now knew, had mislead him about their injuries just so they could play, even though they were still hurting. And, as a result, some of their injuries had been aggravated to the point that they might not be able to play for several weeks.

Ronald Minchew, Blinkey Barber, and John Robert O'Neal played with shoulder injuries; Ed Mixon and Bill Schofill played with knee injuries; Tommy Boney played with an arm injury; and Fred Dollar played with an ankle injury.

Their next game was only a week away, and it was against a team they knew almost nothing about: East Mississippi State Junior College. After that, they were set to play the Middle Georgia Wolverines for the second time. It had only been three weeks since they lost to the Wolverines, and Bowden believed they lost that game because key players were injured and unable to play. He knew they'd have to win their next clash with the Wolverines if they had any hopes of winning the conference championship.

Considering the teams they were facing and the number of injuries, Bowden honestly thought their chances of winning those two games, especially the Middle Georgia game, were slim to none.

Fortunately, his pessimism turned around midweek when he received a call from the East Mississippi coach advising him that they had no choice but to cancel their game because a large number of their players were sick—some even hospitalized—with a very serious Asian flu.

Although disappointed about the game being cancelled, Bowden knew this was a real break for his team because now some of the injured players might have enough time to recuperate before they played the Wolverines.

Bowden and Gibson were also encouraged when they saw how hard all their reserve players were working to prove that they could still win even if the injured players weren't fully recovered by game time. The players working to ease the coaches' minds were: Jim King, Dewitt Galloway, Richard Gamble, and Gaylon Rush, on the line; Wayne Walker at center; and Buzzy Nauright and Bill Black in the backfield.

South Georgia Tigers vs Middle Georgia Wolverines

ON OCTOBER 26, when South Georgia finally squared off against the Middle Georgia Wolverines on the Wolverines' home field, Boney and Schofill were back in the starting lineup, but the other injured first-team players were still questionable, which meant that at least five positions on the starting team were manned by backup players who had little or no game experience at South Georgia.

Strangely enough, this didn't seem to affect anyone's attitude because, apparently, most of the players saw the game as a grudge match that they intended to win to avenge their earlier loss.

As far as the Middle Georgia Wolverines were concerned, they were confident of another victory. They had already defeated all of their conference opponents in earlier matchups, including the Tigers, and they knew that the Tigers still had a number of key players out with injuries.

Once the game started, however, the Wolverines learned very quickly that the game was going to be a hard-fought battle from start to finish. When the first quarter ended scoreless, both teams knew defense was going to be a big factor.

The defensive battle rumbled on until midway through the second quarter when the Tigers got possession of the football on the Wolverines' 39-yard line. They found a few weak seams in the Wolverines seemingly impregnable defense and scored the first touchdown of the game.

Bill Black, who was playing in place of the injured Fred Dollar, carried the ball five times in six plays and picked up 31 of the 39 yards needed to score, including his final 4-yard dash that capped the drive. Elder converted the extra point, and South Georgia led by a score of 7-0 when the first half ended.

The second half continued predominately as a defensive battle, although South Georgia occasionally broke out and demonstrated that they were capable of putting together a consistent running attack, even though they were never able to score again. They did, however, hold on to their 7-point lead until this game was history.

Statistically, the Tigers picked up 16 first downs and gained a total of 280 yards on offense, compared to the Wolverines' 5 first downs and 76 yards rushing. But that didn't mean the Tigers didn't have to deal with that old monkey from the penalty ward hanging around. They lost 105 yards in penalties and at least one touchdown.

Discounting these penalties, Bowden and Gibson were generally pleased with their team's performance, which gave them confidence in their bench strength and their ability to win in the future, even if injuries continued to plague them.

Now the spotlight was on the matchup between the South Georgia Tigers and the Gordon Military College Cadets—a game that had decided the Georgia State Junior College Champions for the past two years.

This year both teams had almost identical records in conference play. Their records boiled down to their games against the Middle Georgia Wolverines. Gordon played the Wolverines one time; the game ended in a 13-13 tie. The Tigers played them twice; the

Wolverines won the first contest by one touchdown, and the Tigers won the second by the same margin.

Fortunately for the Tigers, by the time they started preparing for their game against the Cadets, Bill Schofill was the only injured player who had not completely recuperated. He could play if necessary, but he was still limping because of a nagging leg injury.

Because he didn't want to aggravate any old injuries, Bowden decided to deviate from normal practices the next week and keep the team's preparation light.

By Thursday afternoon, November 7, two days before the all-important contest with the Gordon Cadets, Bowden announced the following starting lineup:

Blinkey Barber ....right end
Bill Schofill ....right tackle
DeWitt Galloway.............right tackle
Ed Mixon........................right guard
Ronald Minchew...............center
Tommy Boney ....left guard
Joe Wallis ....left tackle
Min Skoofalos..................left end
DeWayne Elder.................quarterback
Bobby Pate.......................left halfback
John Robert O'Neal..........right halfback
Bill Black.........................fullback

18

WINNING CHAMPIONSHIPS
COULD BECOME A HABIT

South Georgia Tigers vs Gordon Military Bulldog Cadets

O n November 9, South Georgia's football team defeated
the Gordon Military College Cadets and won another
Georgia State Junior College Championship. For the third year in
a row, the Tigers either won the championship outright or shared
it with Gordon. It was also the third time in as many years that the
Tigers had to defeat the Cadets in their last conference game of the
season to win or share the prestigious title.

The game between the two junior college powerhouses was
played before a packed house at South Georgia's College Field. And,
as anticipated, it was a tremendous battle from the opening kickoff
to the final whistle.

Neither team was able to score in the first half, which was typical
of their past performances in which defense was always an important
factor in the game's outcome.

Even though the scoreboard reflected two big goose eggs, South
Georgia moved the ball almost at will until they got near the Cadets'
goal line. Much like their game the previous week against the Middle
Georgia Wolverines, once they got past their opponent's 20-yard line,
they either hit a wall or made some mental mistake that bogged them
down. Though unable to score, they did gain 134 yards rushing, 12
yards passing, and picked up 9 first downs, compared to the Cadets'
56 yards rushing and 3 first downs.

The second half looked very much like the first until close to the
end of the third quarter when the Tigers managed to take possession
of the football on the Cadets' 27-yard line.

From the 27, the powerful running of Bill Black quickly moved the ball to the Cadets' 9-yard line. Once they reached the 9, they were faced with a fourth-down situation, and because they had struggled on almost every play to advance the ball to where it was, Bowden called on Chico Elder to attempt a 19-yard field goal. Elder split the uprights, and the Tigers took a 3-point lead.

Surprisingly, the Cadets came storming back after receiving the Tigers' kickoff and put together a beautiful 86-yard march that the Tigers were unable to stop. The long drive and touchdown ate up a considerable amount of time and put the Tigers behind by 4 points with less than ten minutes left in the game.

Realizing that time was critical and they were down to their last chance to win the game, the Tigers dug their heels in. They returned a short kickoff back across mid-field to Gordon's 42-yard line, and from there Bobby Pate, Robert Lairsey, and Fred Dollar—running behind the blocking of Minchew, Boney, Mixon, Schofill, Wallis, Barber, and Min Skoofalos—scratched away at the Cadet defense, picking up short, productive yardage, until Dollar finally crashed into the end zone from 4 yards out, scoring the game-winning touchdown.

After taking a 2-point lead, the Tigers kicked off and the Cadets' return team fumbled the football. When the freed ball hit the ground, a host of Tiger linemen, led by Boney, Minchew, and Barber, smothered it. Then the Tigers applied a ball-control offense and used up the last remaining minutes of the game.

Once the game was over, South Georgia was declared the winner of the Georgia State Junior College Championship for the 1957 season.

Neither Bowden nor Gibson would single out any one player, or group of players, for being responsible for the victory. Instead they said it was the result of a total team effort and, therefore, every team member should receive equal credit for it.

When a reporter asked Bowden if he thought winning football championships could become a habit, he replied, "I don't know, but I sure hope so."

This win gave the Tigers a season record of four wins against two defeats and left them with two non-conference games to play to complete the 1957 season.

The last two games were scheduled to be played November 8 in Wadley, Alabama, against the undefeated Southern Union Bison, and November 15 against the Presbyterian College B Team, a four-year school.

South Georgia Tigers vs Southern Union Bison

As THE GAME GOT STARTED in Wadley, Alabama, it didn't take the Tigers long to understand why the Bison were undefeated. They were obviously a well-coached football team with outstanding players.

To add to the Tigers' bad fortune that day, they were playing on the Bison's home field before a very partisan crowd of Bison supporters, and the unfavorable weather conditions were more suitable for boating than football.

With all these negative forces working against them, the Tigers found it hard to stay focused. They struggled most of the game just to stay motivated, which wasn't helped by the fact that they stayed on defense most of the game while the Bison bombarded them relentlessly with a strong passing and running attack.

They were eventually defeated by the Bison 14-zip in a game that was very reminiscent, at least weather-wise, of their first game against West Georgia.

Even though they lost, two players kept them in the game until the final whistle was blown: defensively, Blinkey Barber was a constant source of harassment to the Bison's running backs, and on offense, Robert Lairsey lugged the wet pigskin repeatedly through the slick, slippery mud, picking up critical yardage that kept them competitive. Their efforts were considered a bright spot in a losing cause full of dark moments. One such moment happened when Bobby Pate, who had been a leading ground gainer all season, as well as an outstanding clutch player on defense, broke his leg late in the game.

When asked what he remembered most about the game, Pate said that more than anything else he remembers how miserable the weather and field conditions were. He said when he fell and broke his leg, he ended up face down in about six inches of water and mud, and he thought he was going to drown before he could get up—he was more concerned about getting his head above water and not drowning than he was about whether his leg was broken.

He also said that when he was finally taken to a hospital to have his leg set and placed in a cast, he thought that if he ever considered playing in another football game in this kind of weather, he hoped someone would shoot him before the game started

South Georgia Tigers vs Presbyterian Blue Hose B Team

ON NOVEMBER 15, 1957, the South Georgia Tigers officially closed the door on another football season by defeating the Presbyterian College B team at College Field. This final victory gave the Tigers their third winning season under Bowden's leadership.

To accomplish their last victory, Bowden and Gibson had to rely mainly on reserve players since a large number of the starting team was injured, especially in the backfield where just about every starter was crippled and could only move at half speed.

One backup player in particular stood out, meeting every challenge with flying colors and surprising everyone but himself: Verlyn Giles.

When Giles was suddenly thrust into the starting role to replace Pate, he had very little actual game experience. In fact, the small running back from Jacksonville, Florida, had been on the Tigers' scout team for most of the past two years, rarely getting into a game.

Being on the Tigers' scout team usually meant that he was a third or fourth-string team member, used primarily by the coaches as a stand-in for opponents, to run an opposing team's plays against their own first-team defense—in this case, the best defense in the Georgia State Junior College Conference—as they prepared for their next game.

In most football circles, this is frequently referred to as getting your experience and earning your stripe in the school of hard knocks. In Giles's case, being a tackling dummy for the Tigers' defense for almost two years got him ready for this game, because his performance exceeded everyone's expectations.

Bill Black and Ted Moseley also moved up to the starting team. It was the second time Black had replaced Dollar, and Moseley was in to relieve Elder, who was limping from a knee injury.

Even with injuries sidelining or slowing key players, the Tigers struck first about halfway through the first quarter and scored the first touchdown of the contest.

To successfully score the first TD, Moseley caught the Blue Hose secondary daydreaming and rifled a beautiful 38-yard pass to Verlyn Giles, who charged into the end zone. Elder came into the game to boot the extra point, and the Tigers had a 7-0 lead.

Presbyterian came back in the second quarter and scored a touchdown, but because they missed the extra point, the Tigers held on to a 1-point lead until the first half ended.

When the game resumed in the second half, it was a defensive battle until late in the third quarter when a mix-up in the Tigers' backfield caused a fumble that the Blue Hose recovered close to the Tigers' goal line. It was just what the Blue Hose needed to score their second TD and take a 5-point lead.

After taking the lead, the Blue Hose held the Tigers until late into the final quarter when Bowden used every player remaining in his arsenal. Surprisingly, this helped the Tigers' offense catch fire and move the football with more consistency.

In this last ditch effort, Black, Giles, and Lairsey moved the football 60 yards to the Blue Hose 1-yard line before Elder pushed it into the end zone behind the blocking of Minchew and Boney. After Elder booted the extra point, the Tigers held on to a 14-12 lead until the game was history.

They only won by 2 points, but statistically, the Tigers were a much better team. The offense picked up 21 first downs and 385 yards rushing compared to Presbyterian's 15 first downs and 242 yards.

The win gave the Tigers another successful season, highlighted by winning the Georgia State Junior College Conference Championship. Although they had to share the previous year's conference title, this year it was very clear that the title belonged to the Tigers alone.

After the end of the season, Jerome "Blinkey" Barber, a player that Coach Bowden had moved from fullback to end, was notified that he had been selected as a member of the Williamson's Junior College All-American team, which was the highest honor any junior college football player could receive at that time.

Coach Bowden was also honored. He was selected by the Atlanta Journal Constitution Sportswriters' Association to be Georgia's junior college "Coach of the Year." Seven of his players were also selected to the association's all-state team: three on the first team and four on the second team. Barber led South Georgia's selections on the first team, and Schofill and Pate joined him. Those selected for the second team were: Boney, Minchew, Elder, and Dollar. Being selected to the all-state team was one of the most sought-after honors in the state's junior college conference, second only to being selected to the Williamson's All-American team.

The Tigers' football championship and all the individual honors the players received were just part of one of the most memorable years of athletic accomplishment in the history of South Georgia College.

After the 1957-1958 school year was completed, the South Georgia Tigers stood alone as the reigning conference champions in three sports: football, track, and baseball. In addition to those championship titles, they were the runners-up in the conference's golf finals and placed fourth in the state's basketball tournament.

The most amazing part of this story is that every team, with the exception of the golf team, was coached by either Bowden or Gibson. Bowden coached the baseball team and Gibson coached the basketball and track teams.

19

THE START OF A
DIFFERENT KIND OF SEASON

*F*or *all practical purposes*, the Tigers' 1958 football season started in March of that year when Bowden turned spring training into a tryout camp for aspiring high school footballers who wanted to play for the Tigers. This certainly wasn't the first time he had tried this, but, by 1958, he had perfected it and turned it into the Tigers' biggest recruiting source.

The real significance of this tryout wasn't felt until September 8, when the Tigers' preseason camp began. That's when Bowden estimated that about 80 percent of all of their new players were there because of the spring tryouts.

Several newcomers were from as far away as Indiana, Pennsylvania, and Virginia.

Most notable were:

Hueland Hill, a 160-pound "Class A" high school all-state quarterback from Sylvania, Georgia

Hubert Miller, a 180-pound fullback from Quitman, Georgia

Ray Parker and David Hughes, two 190-pound guards from Miami Edison High School in Miami, Florida

Tommy Heath, a 210-pound tackle from Soperton, Georgia

Ken Dean, a 225-pound tackle from Tallahassee, Florida

David Powell, a 190-pound high school all-state center from Jacksonville, Florida

Larry Gaylor, a 195-pound high school all-state fullback from Winchester, Indiana

James Jacobelli, a 190-pound quarterback from Jeanette, Pennsylvania

Raymond Landrum, a 175-pound fullback from Lyons, Georgia

Mike Doyal, a 180-pound guard from Albany, Georgia

Billy Benton, a 155-pound halfback from Lyons, Georgia

Bonwell Royal, a 180-pound guard from Douglas, Georgia

Carl Shepherd, a 185-pound fullback from Douglas, Georgia

Bobby Jackson, a 160-pound halfback from Forsyth, Georgia

In addition to these recent high school graduates, there were also several outstanding transfers from some major universities.

One such individual was Sam Smith, a guard who played his freshman year at the University of Florida. Another one was George Versprille, a running back who grew up in Norfolk, Virginia, but played his freshman year of football at Florida State University. Versprille's transferred to South Georgia with the unusual distinction that he had scored two touchdowns against the Tigers the year before when the Tigers lost to FSU's B Team.

Two other outstanding transfers were Wayne Jackson, a center who played his freshman year at the University of Tennessee, and Preston Nix, a lineman who played his first year of college football at the University of South Carolina.

In addition to this group of impressive newcomers, fifteen players from the Tigers' 1957 championship squad returned:

Min Skoofalos, a 190-pound end from Green Cove Springs, Florida

Jim King, a 210-pound end from Albany, Georgia

Jim Alvarez, a 180-pound end from Jacksonville, Florida

Davis Parrish, a 185-pound end from Statesboro, Georgia

Turk Gibbs, a 210-pound tackle from St. Augustine, Florida

Tillman Norris, a 185-pound end from Adel, Georgia

Richard Gamble, a 170-pound guard from Atlanta, Georgia

DeWitt Galloway, a 210-pound tackle from Apalachicola, Florida

Jimmy Norton, a 160-pound guard from Cuthbert, Georgia

Donald Sellers, a 195-end from Wadsworth, Ohio

B.B. Braddock, a 185-pound quarterback from Belle Glade, Florida

Robert Lairsey, a 190-pound halfback from Waycross, Georgia

Fred Dollar, a 180-pound fullback from Cairo, Georgia

Bill Black, a 180-pound fullback from Sylvania, Georgia, and

Joe Sears, a 165-pound halfback from Alma, Georgia

After Bowden had a chance to combine all the new candidates with the returning players and watch them practice as a team, he got really excited about the approaching season, believing this was the best group of prospects he'd seen since beginning his tenure at South Georgia. All that talent would surely give the team a good chance of winning another conference championship.

His initial excitement grew when he realized that, unlike past seasons, their 1958 schedule included only junior college opponents, except one game. In the past, they had to play two or three four-year college teams just to have an eight or nine game schedule.

The one exception was a game against Presbyterian College's B team. Presbyterian College was a small four-year college, and the Tigers had played and defeated them the year before.

The excitement spread among all the players until the temperature in southern Georgia got a little hotter, the hitting got a little harder, and the dust flew a little higher. But it didn't take long for some of the initial excitement to fade once reality crept in.

The biggest problem was the weather, especially among the players from the northern parts of the country who were having a hard time getting acclimated to the hot, humid temperatures in the South.

The first two weeks of practice during preseason camp, which included two practices a day in temperatures exceeding ninety degrees, affected players whether they were from the North or the South. Some surely suffered from heat exhaustion. And because heat exhaustion wasn't fully understood at the time, it was probably the catalyst for a multitude of injuries that eventually affected the overall well-being of the entire team.

Once the downward spiral started, Bowden spent a large amount of his time taking care of injured players and juggling the few healthy ones he had left so he could keep every position filled as their first game drew near. The injuries had a detrimental effect and dampened the team's spirit and initial excitement, which increased Bowden's concerns about their future.

By the time the preseason camp was over, there were only thirty-six players remaining on the Tigers' 1958 team:

NAME	POSITION	WEIGHT	NUMBER
Jimmy Thompson	End	180	13
Herbert Miller	End	185	33
David Parrish	End	187	37
Jim Alvarez	End	190	36
Min Skoofalos	End	195	50
George Faircloth	End	179	19
Bill Lesky	End	175	18
Preston Nix	Tackle	210	37
Sanford Brunson	Tackle	225	55
Richard Finley	Tackle	212	31
Turk Gibbs	Tackle	210	56
David Hughes	Guard	196	40
Ray Parker	Guard	190	32
Sam Smith	Guard	200	51
Bonwell Royal	Guard	183	39
Bob Jones	Guard	200	34
Jimmy Norton	Guard	170	33
Harold Crews	Guard	185	10
Wayne Jackson	Center	235	44
Don Sellers	Center	215	27

Harry Brown	Center	168	35
Hueland Hill	Quarterback	158	59
B.B. Braddock	Quarterback	186	53
James Jacobelli	Quarterback	190	51
Fred Dollar	Halfback	178	47
Billy Benton	Halfback	155	46
John Porterfield	Halfback	175	24
Tony Bell	Halfback	150	21
George Versprille	Halfback	185	48
Robert Lairsey	Halfback	198	35
Bobby Jackson	Halfback	158	20
Joe Sears	Halfback	170	14
Bill Black	Fullback	185	12
Larry Gaylor	Fullback	190	42
Carl Shepherd	Fullback	180	17

It was during their first game against the Georgia Military College Bulldogs that the depth of the injury problem was discovered. The Tigers quickly fell behind the Bulldogs in the first half by a score of 7-0. They struggled until late in the third quarter when they evened the score. In the late stages of the final quarter, they scored again and came away with the victory. The success of their comeback was mostly due to George Verprille and Bill Black's hard running and a strong defensive effort led by Don Sellers.

Even though they won the game, Bowden knew they hadn't played well, and during their next week of practice, he told his players they'd have to play a lot better against the Gordon Military Cadets if they expected to win. He knew that the team that avoided mental mistakes, penalties, and fumbles in that game would be the team that won.

Today, this rhetoric is much more commonplace than it was in the 1950s, but despite his philosophy being ahead of the curve, the Tigers were not.

In their game against the Cadets, the Tigers lost the football six times because of fumbles, which increased their tendency to make mental mistakes. As a result, they were penalized 105 yards, which cancelled out some of the best running efforts of George Versprille, Robert Lairsey, and Bill Black. Bowden's prediction that fumbles, mental mistakes, and penalties would determine the winner of the game was right on the money—the Tigers lost by a score of 20-0.

After the game, Bowden told reporters that his players had played as individuals, not as a team; consequently, they lost to a better team.

In their third game, against the Middle Georgia Wolverines, the Tigers' offense showed some improvement, but it was still their defense that kept them competitive.

The defense, however, wasn't enough to change the outcome of the game, which ended in a 0-0 deadlock. Even though their offense outgained Middle Georgia's offense in rushing and passing, the Tigers still couldn't get on the scoreboard, which was mostly due to the number of penalties they received. In total they racked up 85 yards in penalties compared to the Wolverines' 15. They also continued to have problems finding the handle on the football, turning it over to the Wolverines four times because of fumbles.

Bowden knew they could have defeated the Wolverines if they had just been able to overcome their biggest liabilities: penalties and fumbles. But on the bright side, he and Gibson were relieved to see their players finally working together as a team and the offense moving the ball with more confidence and consistency.

The brightest spot in their offense was the performance of their freshman quarterback, Hueland Hill. Hill was playing with a lot more confidence than he had played with in the first two games, and as a consequence, the entire offense was performing better. On defense, both coaches singled out Turk Gibbs as their outstanding defensive player, crediting him with seventeen individual tackles.

After completing their first three games, their record stood at one win, one loss, and one tie. With this record, Bowden knew their chance of retaining the conference championship was very slim. In his mind, their only hope was to win all six of their remaining games. To do that they would have to defeat Georgia Military College again, as well as Gordon and Middle Georgia, who defeated and tied them in their first matches.

Their fourth game of the season was a non-conference game that was scheduled to be played in Lyons, Georgia, against Presbyterian College's B team from South Carolina. Lyons was a small rural town in the south central part of the state. The situation surrounding this game was somewhat unusual because it was being sponsored by a local civic organization and being played on a neutral field. The Lions Club was using the Thursday night game on October 16 to raise funds for several civic projects.

Because of this, Lyons rolled out the red carpet for Bowden and the Tigers, including a reception and a lot of fanfare on the day of the game. With all the attention given to the team, anyone who didn't know better would think South Georgia was playing at home.

Once the game got underway, Bowden did his best to keep the excitement going and to show the citizens of Lyons that the Tigers appreciated their support. Reaching way down into his bag of tricks, he produced a play that took South Georgia into the end zone on their first play of the game. To make it even sweeter, he used Billy Benton, a high school star from Lyons who was now playing for the Tigers, to score the touchdown.

After the opening kickoff, Bowden hid Benton in plain view on the field in front of the Tigers' bench while the rest of the team lined up on the 41-yard line. It was called a lonesome-end play, and it was sometimes used against a defensive team that didn't realize the offensive team only had ten players lined up on the ball.

Once the ball was snapped, James Jacobelli threw a perfect strike to lonesome-end Benton, who hadn't been noticed by the Presbyterian defense until the ball was thrown. Once Benton caught the ball, he took off on a 59-yard sprint to the end zone, which brought the Lyons spectators to their feet in uncontrolled jubilation. After that they cheered every Tiger success for the remainder of the game, which kept the Tigers motivated enough to score two more TDs and a field goal before winning the game 22-0.

The Tigers' offense showed tremendous improvement throughout the game, but it was still their defensive play that gave them the winning edge.

Throughout most of the game, the Tigers' defense kept the Presbyterian Blue Hose backed up against their own goal line. Bowden said after the game, "This was our first real team effort, and I hope it's the turning point that we needed to finish the season on a winning note." He said every one of his players who saw action played an outstanding game.

This victory gave the Tigers their second win of the season and seemed to rejuvenate team spirit.

Since the game was played on a Thursday night, the Tigers got a much-needed long week to prepare for their next game against the West Georgia Braves on October 25. Bowden hoped the long week would give his players the extra time they needed to finally recuperate from injuries that had plagued them most of the season.

On October 25, after a long week of light workouts, Bowden was confident that his team was finally ready—physically and mentally—to play the kind of football he believed they were capable of playing.

He also knew that if he was wrong and they lost their next game, they had run out of excuses. Like the old cliché says, "The time has come to either play ball or get off the field." Bowden sent his team onto the field to face the West Georgia Braves with a final warning: their fate was in their own hands. Win, lose, or draw, they would be the ones responsible for the end results.

Taking his words as motivation, the South Georgia Tigers immediately combined a powerful running attack and an accurate passing game with their most reliable strength: their defensive play. By combining their strengths, they steamrolled to a 28–0 victory over the

West Georgia squad, a team many had believed to be the best team the Braves had fielded in several years.

To win the game, the Tigers scored a touchdown in every quarter, capping off drives of 70, 65, 52, and 65 yards. The defense played its usual outstanding game and held the visiting Braves' offense to 4 first downs, no points scored, and 37 yards gained.

In the first quarter, after starting from their own 30-yard line, George Versprille, Fred Dollar, and Bill Black bulled their way into the Braves' end zone, scoring the first 6 points of the game for the Tigers.

James Jacobelli heaved a beautiful 32-yard pass to Jim Alvarez in the second quarter, which put the Tigers very close to the Braves' goal line. On their next play, starting from inside the Braves' 5-yard line, Black charged through the line of scrimmage and across the goal line to score their second touchdown. Their third touchdown came in the third quarter after Jacobelli uncorked another beautiful pass to Min Skoofalos, putting the Tigers and the football on the Braves' 2-yard line. Once they were on the 2-yard line, Fred Dollar fought his way around the left side of the line and into pay dirt for the score.

In the final quarter, the Tigers scored their last touchdown after blocking a Braves' punt inside their 30-yard line. To bring their last drive to a climax, Hueland Hill, who had replaced Jacobelli at quarterback, unleashed a steaming pass to Hubert Miller in the Braves' end zone, giving the Tigers an impressive 28-0 victory.

The win was one everyone could be happy about because the Tigers had finally played sixty minutes of almost perfect football. The wide smiles on Bowden and Gibson's faces when they strolled off the field after the game was evidence enough to conclude that they were looking forward to the rest of this season.

After the game, Bowden was hesitant to say too much about their season so far, or about what he expected in their next four games, but he did admit that this had certainly been a different kind of season.

20

THE BIGGEST SURPRISE OF THE
1958 FOOTBALL SEASON

After the Tigers convincingly defeated the Braves, Bowden felt his players' confidence come creeping back, which made him think they had finally turned the corner. He also thought that maybe, just maybe, if they continued playing the same way for the remainder of the season, they could still be the conference champions. It would be a monumental accomplishment because they would have to win every game remaining on their schedule, which were all rematches against their toughest conference opponents: Georgia Military College, Middle Georgia College, and Gordon Military College. One slip-up or bad game against any one of these teams would eliminate them. If they stayed healthy though, they might be able to pull it off.

Their first hurdle was to defeat the Georgia Military Bulldogs on November 1. Bowden knew they were fortunate to have the home field advantage, but even so, he suspected this game would be the toughest one left on their schedule. The Tigers had barely won their first game with the Bulldogs, and the Bulldogs were better now than they were in the beginning of the season. Also, because the Tigers won the first time around, Bowden expected the Bulldogs to come back fired up and ready to revenge their loss.

Knowing the game was going to be a real cat-and-dog fight, Bowden prepared his team as if they'd be playing a championship playoff game, which it very well could've been. The game was slated as the main attraction of South Georgia's homecoming festivities, and Bowden hoped this would give his players the extra incentive they needed to win, knowing that it had helped in the past.

On Friday October 31—after the Tigers had completed a tough week of preparation—Colonel R.A. Horne, GMC's president, telephoned President Smith at South Georgia to notify him that they would not be able to play their scheduled game because of an outbreak of flu among the Bulldog players.

When Smith told Bowden about Colonel Horne's call, Bowden was stunned and upset. This was the second time in two years something like this had happened; the first being the year before when Mississippi State Junior College had cancelled for the same reason.

Once he got over the initial shock, Bowden's imagination changed gears. He got together with Ronnie Kelley and Stumpy Franklin, a couple of his boys from the 1955 and 1956 football teams, who had come to South Georgia for the homecoming festivities, and they came up with the idea of putting together an alumni team to play in place of the Bulldogs. It was an idea no one in his right mind would even dream of today, much less expect to happen, but to Bowden and his boys, it just seemed natural under the circumstances.

With less than twenty-four hours to put together a team of former South Georgia players, Bowden and Coach Gibson got busy rounding up enough extra uniforms to outfit twenty players. While they were doing that, Kelley and Franklin went scouting for enough alumni players to make up a team.

A buzz rippled across campus and the city of Douglas as, all of a sudden, former South Georgia players started coming from everywhere. The next morning, eighteen former South Georgia footballers met with Bowden at the gymnasium, and together they divided up old uniforms and developed a game plan. By then Bowden had decided he would coach the alumni team and Gibson would coach the current Tiger team.

The group of past players, who some referred to as the South Georgia Misfits, spent what time they had left before the game trying on uniforms and deciding who would play what position. A few of them even tossed a football around a little—something most of them hadn't done for awhile.

Included in this group was:

Hoke Smith, a member of the 1954 and 1955 teams
Rosby Mulkey, a member of the 1955 and 1956 teams
David Hill, a member of the 1953 team
Stumpy Franklin, a member of the 1955 and 1956 teams
Ed Mixon, a member of the 1956 and 1957 teams
Jerry Holland, a member of the 1955 and 1956 teams
J.C. Rowe, a member of the 1951 team
Roger Wilkinson, a member of the 1955 and 1956 teams
Louis Studdard, a member of the 1955 and 1956 teams
Chico Elder, a member of the 1956 and 1957 teams
Ronnie Kelley, a member of the 1954 and 1955 teams
Verlyn Giles, a member of the 1956 and 1957 teams
Waymon Vickers, a member of the 1956 and 1957 teams
Everett Graham, a member of the 1955 and 1956 teams
Vernon Brinson, a member of the 1955 and 1956 teams
Blinkey Barber, a member of the 1955, 1956 (red shirted), and 1957 teams
Ronnie Harrison, a member of the 1957 team
Buzzy Nauright, a member of the 1956 (red shirted) and 1957 teams

A few hours later, the matchup between the ragtag South Georgia Misfits and the current Tiger team got underway. Surprising to almost everyone, it was one of the most exciting homecoming football games in South Georgia's history, especially once everyone realized that former stars, including four former junior college All-American's, had donned their battle gear one more time for ole SGC. It was the only time anyone at South Georgia had ever heard of something like this happening at any college or university.

This was no exhibition game either; the two teams went at each other like the national championship was at stake. Ronnie Kelley was heard after the game saying that the first time he was hit, he thought every bone in his body had broken, but after he realized he was still in one piece and his body adjusted to the shock of being knocked around again, it was a lot of fun. Of course, the next day he could hardly get out of bed.

During the game, it was obvious that conditioning, or in the case of the Misfits, the lack of conditioning, and the fact that they hadn't practiced for some time, in some cases years, was going to be a huge disadvantage to the alumni. But it didn't keep them from trying to make the game as exciting as they could for themselves and their fellow alumni in the stands.

Using every trick play in his playbook, as well as a few that he and his players made up on the sidelines, Bowden kept the game interesting for everyone involved, including the spectators. It was even occasionally challenging for the current Tiger team.

Even though the alumni never got across the goal line—the final score was 13-0—the game was a lot closer than anyone thought it would be. The Tigers probably didn't play with as much enthusiasm as they would have played their regularly scheduled contest against the Bulldogs, but they did seem to enjoy clashing with some of the older players. The bottom line was that both teams gave a good accounting of themselves, and under the circumstances, they made what could have been a disastrous homecoming event, a huge success.

Once all the hoopla surrounding the alumni game was over, Bowden and his team got back to business and got serious about their next scheduled game.

When the Georgia Military Bulldogs forfeited their game, the Tigers earned another win, making their season record 4-1-1, which put them back in the mix for the conference championship. It also made their next game on November 6 against the Middle Georgia Wolverines even more important.

Because their game against the Wolverines was on a Thursday night, Bowden knew he and his players had a lot to do in a short period of time to get ready. As in the past, the game would be played in Cochran on the Wolverines' home field in front of a Middle Georgia homecoming crowd. Middle Georgia also had one of the best defenses in the conference, and Bowden knew they were in for a fierce fight and would have their hands full all night.

In five conference games, the Wolverines had only allowed two touchdowns to be scored on them, and those two touchdowns had been scored through the air. Bowden knew this, and recalled that their first game had ended in a scoreless tie, so he expected that his players would have to play flawless football for four quarters if they wanted to win.

Since he believed it was too late in the season to make any major changes, and because not playing as a team and making mental mistakes had been a big problem for the Tigers in their first meeting with the Wolverines, Bowden spent a large part of the team's preparation time emphasizing the importance of teamwork and mental toughness.

It turned out to be precisely the type of game that Bowden expected. It was a tough, hard-fought, exciting contest between two teams determined to win. Every play was crucial—just one mistake or miscue could easily have changed the game's direction.

Fortunately for the Tigers, they played their best game of the year, and in doing so, they topped the Wolverines in every department, including the final score, which was 16–13.

Though Bowden and his players had been led to believe that the Wolverines' line was the best in the conference, it was the Tigers' linemen who made the difference and, in the end, won the game for them. Led by Turk Gibbs, Min Skoofalos, Jimmy Norton, Sam Smith, and Don Sellers, they turned in their finest performance of the year and held the Wolverines' offense to just 144 yards rushing.

The offense did its job as well, opening up the Wolverines' defense enough to allow their runners to gain 285 yards, which none of the Wolverines' previous five opponents had been able to do.

In the backfield, jolting George Versprille and big Robert Lairsey, along with Fred Dollar and Hueland Hill, kept the Tigers' offense rolling by averaging over 5 yards per carry. They also managed to score two touchdowns on the ground, which was another season first against the stingy Wolverine defense. Not only did they work together as a team to accomplish great things against the Wolverines, they also maintained mental toughness: the Tigers were only penalized once during the entire game.

After putting the game behind them, the Tigers had a long week to get ready for their non-conference matchup against the Southern Union Bison from Wadley, Alabama. Their only previous meeting with the Bison was in 1957 when the Bison won the game 14-0 in a rainstorm on their home field. This year the game was going to be played at South Georgia's College Field, and Bowden hoped that better weather and the home field advantage would help them come out on top.

As hoped, Bowden was rewarded when, on November 15, the Tigers immediately exerted control over the game and eventually romped over the Bison by a very impressive 54-24 score.

Fred Dollar set the pace for the Tigers by scoring three touchdowns and rushing for 128 yards. The other big gainers for the Tigers were George Versprille, Bill Black, Robert Lairsey, and Carl Sheppard. In total, the Tigers gained 383 yards on offense and picked up 14 first downs.

In the aerial department, James Jacobelli and Hueland Hill were the big guns for the Tigers, while Bobby Jackson and Min Skoofalos were generally on the receiving end of their passes.

The mighty Tiger line played another outstanding game. Most notable in this wall of human flesh were Don Sellers, Sam Smith, Ray Parker, Preston Nix, Turk Gibbs, Min Skoofalos, and Jim Alvarez.

According to Bowden, these linemen demonstrated once again that they were the backbone of the team.

After finishing off Southern Union with their best offensive show of the season, the Tigers had only one more conference game before wrapping up their season. As was tradition, it was the big one against the Gordon Military Cadets for the conference championship.

Since 1955, when Bowden first took the helm of South Georgia's football program, it had always been their last game against the Cadets that decided who would wear the conference crown for another year.

Since the Tigers had lost their second game of the year to the Cadets and tied the Middle Georgia Wolverines in their third game, their conference record coming into the final game was six wins, one tie, and one loss. The Cadets' record also included one tie and one loss. Oddly enough, their tie game was also against the Wolverines, who they only played once.

Bowden, quoted in a local newspaper before the game, said, "If we can stop their passing attack and hold our penalties and fumbles down, we have a good chance of winning."

Bowden knew the Tigers' line was as good as any other in the conference and that the Tigers had three running backs who were without equal: George Versprille and Fred Dollar, both of whom were averaging over 6 yards per carry, and Bill Black, who was frequently called upon to pick up the hard yardage. Black wasn't far behind Versprille and Dollar in yards per carry.

On November 22, after a tough but spirited week of preparation, the South Georgia Tigers and the Gordon Military Bulldog Cadets lined up against each other in Douglas, in what had become an annual ritual, to decide the best of the best in junior college football in the state of Georgia.

As history predicted, it was one of the most grueling contests of the year in the Georgia State Junior College Conference, and victory eventually went to the team that was able to avoid making the last mistake, or was able to capitalize on their opponent's last mistake.

202 ·//· Jim Bowen

The Cadets took the opening kickoff and set a seemingly unstoppable drive in motion—unstoppable, that is, until they got to the Tigers' 38-yard line and a host of Tiger tacklers separated the football from a Cadet runner. The turnover gave the Tigers their first big break of the game; immediately after that Fred Dollar ran the ball 51 yards to the Cadets' 13-yard line.

Two plays later, George Versprille raced across the goal line from 11 yards out, scoring the first touchdown of the game.

As was expected, the game quickly settled into an intense defensive brawl. The standoff lasted until Gordon's offense caught fire midway through the second quarter as they mounted their best offensive drive of the game.

Balancing a strong running game with a successful passing attack, the Cadets didn't slow down until they scored their first touchdown, converted the extra point, and took a 7-6 lead.

The game reverted to deadlock, and the next few minutes were spent exchanging punts, which lasted until the Tigers grabbed a short one in the middle of the field and took advantage of it. Versprille gobbled up 43 yards in two plays and moved the ball to the Cadets' 11-yard line. From there, the Tigers had about 90 seconds to get into the end zone and take the lead before the first half ended.

As the clock ticked off the last few seconds of the half, Versprille made two desperate attempts to get the ball across the goal line, but on both tries he came up short, sending the Tigers to the locker room trailing by one point when the half ended.

When the third quarter began, both teams came back to the field reenergized, and their offenses moved the football with impressive regularity. Neither, however, was able to add any more points to the scoreboard.

The seesaw battle continued into the final quarter until the Tigers' forced the Cadets to punt the football from deep inside their own territory. When their punt came down around the 50-yard marker, it was fumbled by the Tigers' deep return man and recovered by the Cadets.

The Tigers were in another difficult situation, and now time was critical. Even though they held the Cadets and forced them to punt again after three downs, they were driven back to their own 10-yard line.

Because time was running out and they were still deep inside their own territory, the Tigers rushed their plays and made mistakes. The final nail in the coffin was a hurried pass that was intercepted by Gordon and run back across the goal line for their second touchdown, which put the Cadets ahead of the Tigers 13–6 and gave them the victory and conference crown.

The unfortunate part of this story for the Tigers was that they outplayed the Cadets for most of the game, which was, except for the final score, easily verifiable by the game statistics. They picked up 12 first downs compared to Gordon's 8 and gained 283 yards on offense compared to Gordon's 187. They were also penalized less than Gordon—85 yards compared to 150, which was remarkable for the Tigers—and they lost the football fewer times in turnovers: 2 to Gordon's 3. Their 2 turnovers, however, happened at the most critical time of the game: the last few minutes. It was those last two turnovers that cost them the championship, but Bowden praised his players anyway for the way they hung together in the latter part of the season.

Everyone associated with the Tigers' football team, as well as their supporters, was surprised and disappointed that they didn't win the championship, but Bowden was probably more surprised than anyone.

When the season began, he believed the players on this team were the best group of players he had coached since taking the job at South Georgia, and he had expected to win another championship.

In 1958, though, Bowden was still a young man perfecting his trade. If anyone asked him about preseason predictions today, he'd probably say that he learned very early in his coaching career that preseason predictions are very fragile at best and generally not worth the time it takes to make them, no matter who is making them.

Losing the championship was a shock, but it was nothing compared to the surprise President Smith revealed to him later in the school year when they got together to discuss the school's athletic budget.

Since Bowden had been South Georgia's athletic director, no annual budget meeting had been out of the ordinary or surprising. This one, however, was different. President Smith informed him that the school's trustees had decided to discontinue football at South Georgia. According to Smith's explanation, there wasn't enough money in the school's budget to support the football program.

Bowden could hardly believe what he was hearing. After building a winning program that included three championships, he didn't understand how this could be happening. But once he got beyond his initial shock, he realized he had just learned another important lesson about college football: money to support a football program is much more important than winning games or championships, although it is generally believed that winning is necessary to gather that support.

Smith asked Bowden to stay on as South Georgia's athletic director and head baseball coach, but football was his dream, so he left Smith's office in a daze without committing himself. All he could think about at that moment was that he'd finally figured out how to build a winning football program, and then, without a hint of warning, the whole program was jerked away from him.

He walked back to his office thinking about what had just happened and what he and his family had gone through in the last few years just so he could live his dream of being a head football coach. He couldn't help but feel despondent and disappointed. It seemed to him that this was the end of his football-coaching career. But what he should've realized was that God still had a plan for his life, and that this was only the end of the beginning and not the beginning of the end as he was thinking.

When he finally reached his office, he could hardly hold back his tears. Through the blur, he noticed a letter on his desk from Dr. Leslie Wright, the new president of Howard College in Birmingham, Alabama. At first he couldn't imagine why Dr. Wright was contacting him. He assumed it was because he was a graduate of Howard; maybe the school was notifying its graduates that Dr. Wright had been selected as the new president, or maybe it was just one of those letters to alumni soliciting funds.

Never in his wildest imaginings did he think that Dr. Wright would be writing to offer him the head football coach job at his alma mater. But that's exactly what the letter was about.

It was a brief and simple letter asking Bowden if he was interested in becoming the head coach at Howard. When he read the letter, he realized that often when things look their darkest, there is an opportunity lurking in the shadows. In this instance, it was an opportunity of a lifetime, or as Mike Bynum quoted Bowden in his book *Bound for Glory*, it was "like a miracle sent from Heaven."

The thing that made the offer so amazing was that it was the same job he had applied for four years earlier, before coming to South Georgia, but because of his age and lack of experience, he had been denied the job by the former president at Howard. Nineteen fifty-eight certainly was a year of surprises for Bowden, and the letter from Dr. Wright was the biggest surprise of all.

After reading Wright's letter, it didn't take Bowden long to accept her offer and return to his alma mater. When he left South Georgia, at the end of the 1958 school year, he took thirteen players from South Georgia's 1958 team with him, including Bonwell Royal, Carl Sheppard, Richard Finley, Jimmy Thompson, Bobby Jackson, George Versprille, and Robert Lairsey. These young men quickly became the building blocks of his first team at Howard College.

*W*ith the exception of the thirteen players Bowden took with him to Howard College, he had very little contact—other than an occasional Christmas card or coincidental meeting—with other former South Georgia players for several years after he left.

Most had gone on to play at some other college or university or were busy building their own careers and were scattered across several states.

This separation lasted for almost fifteen years, until a few of those former players got together and started talking about bygone days at South Georgia and how playing for Coach Bowden had affected their lives.

At first, only a few made up the group: Roger Wilkinson, Bull Smith, Jerry Holland, Ronnie Kelley, and Jimmy Bowen, all of whom were still living in Georgia. Later, their numbers grew, and the closeness that they had experienced as teammates playing football for the South Georgia Tigers was rekindled.

Later, in 1972, a couple years after Bowden became the head coach at the University of West Virginia and his team accepted an invitation to play in the Peach Bowl in Atlanta against North Carolina State, a group of former Tigers planned a get-together to coincide with the game. One of them contacted Bowden, notified him of their intentions, and invited him to join them if time permitted.

They were surprised when, the day before the Peach Bowl game, Bowden broke away from his busy schedule and the many obligations he had associated with the bowl game, and joined them at their motel for a couple hours.

This was the first face-to-face contact most of them had had with Bowden since he left South Georgia. And even though it had been at least fifteen years, he remembered every one of them and was genuinely interested in what they had been doing since their last contact. Later, before he left, he invited everyone who could make it to come by the Mountaineers' locker room after the game to meet some of the boys who were playing for him now.

Several accepted his invitation and met Bowden on the field after the game before walking with him to the locker room. Once inside with the team, they saw firsthand that the character of this man they remembered so fondly and loved and respected so much had not changed. Even though his team had lost their game by what some fans and sportswriters considered an embarrassing 49–13 score—and he had every right to be disappointed and upset—his actions never showed any discouragement.

Instead, with a big smile on his face, he took the former South Georgia players around and introduced them to his current team like they were his prodigal sons. A few minutes later, he called all his West Virginia players together to talk to them. The first thing he said was something like this: "Boys, I think that before we do anything else, we need to take a minute and thank God for giving us the opportunity that we had today to play in this bowl game, and also for helping us to get through it without anyone getting seriously hurt." He then got down on one knee, bowed his head, and led them in a prayer.

It was typical behavior for Bowden, but it was an amazing testament to his character and faith that many people have never had the opportunity or privilege to witness. The dressing room at the time was wet and steamy and filled with more than sixty young men, downhearted by their loss. But they didn't hesitate to gather around this remarkable man, their coach and leader, who was down on his knees giving thanks to God for every one of them and for the many blessings He had provided them as a group and a team.

They stood surrounding him or knelt down with their heads bowed, in silence and in various stages of dress. The only sound anyone could hear was Bowden's humble voice in prayer.

To those few former South Georgia players privileged enough to be in that room that day, this was just another example of how Bowden consistently and persistently used his faith and his position as a football coach to demonstrate to an untold number of young men what's really important in life.

Three years later, in 1975, when the University of West Virginia returned to the Peach Bowl for their second clash with North Carolina State, some of the South Georgia boys met with Bowden again.

In 1976, after Bowden accepted the head football coach job at Florida State University, more South Georgia players could visit more often. In fact, Bowden made it easy for them with instructions to his administrative assistant, Sue Hall. He told her that if any of his boys from South Georgia ever called, he wanted to be notified as soon as possible.

With the increased frequency of their contact, some South Georgians even referred recruits to Florida State (this, of course, was back when recruiting for Florida State was more difficult than it is today, before the best high school players in the country wanted to play for the Seminoles), which led to closer relationships with Bowden. Many even became Florida State fans. The former Tigers got together as often as possible at Seminoles' games, where watching the game was important, but the real purpose was to celebrate their camaraderie and continue to renew their friendships.

These informal get-togethers eventually led to the first organized reunion of South Georgia football players in Jacksonville Beach, Florida, in 1983. Twenty to twenty-five former players made it to the first reunion. Bowden wasn't able to attend because by then he was a highly sought-after celebrity, and his time had to be scheduled several months in advance.

A couple years after that reunion, Ape Adams, Bull Smith, Ronnie Kelley, and Doodlebug Evans, who were all in the Elberton, Georgia area, decided they wanted to have another reunion, but this time they wanted Bowden and as many of their former teammates as possible to attend. With those goals in mind, they organized themselves into a reunion committee and designated Kelley as their chairman.

Kelley contacted Cynthia Wynn Shuman, a former cheerleader at South Georgia, and solicited her assistance. Cynthia had maintained close contact with many former classmates, so she started compiling a list and contacting as many people as she could. Her outreach had a domino effect, and she quickly added more and more names to her list.

While Cynthia's list was growing, Kelley contacted Bowden, explained the plan, and asked him if he thought he would ever be able to attend. Bowden said he was interested and would try to find a date that was open on his schedule. He even suggested that maybe the reunion could be held in Douglas, close to South Georgia College.

Anyone who knows anything about Bowden's schedule knows that finding an open date was a difficult undertaking. It took Sue Hall and Kelley more than a year to find and announce the selected date. By then, Kelley and his committee had at least fifty commitments from former South Georgia players, not including their wives, family members, and friends they wanted to bring along.

On the first Friday of June 1987, Bowden and his boys from South Georgia College converged on the Holiday Inn in Douglas for their first reunion with their former coach—the man who had a profound influence on their lives. It was also the first time many of them had a chance to step back in time and recapture the closeness they had as teammates three decades before while playing for Bowden.

When Bowden and his wife, Ann, arrived at the Holiday Inn, he went inside to register and learned that many of his former players were already congregating around the motel's pool. The pool was behind the motel, almost directly behind the registration desk, so he walked over to a window that overlooked the pool to see if he could recognize anyone.

After staring out the window for a couple minutes, he walked back to his car in the front of the motel and told Ann that the boys were supposed to be outside by the pool, but when he looked, all he saw were a bunch of old men. Ann had to remind him that it had been thirty years since he last saw most of them, and it was very likely that they had gotten a little older. He seemed a little shocked, realizing that time doesn't stand still for anyone, and exclaimed, "My boys are old men now."

He's been reminded of that brief moment of confusion many times since then, to which he usually responds, "They were my first boys, and they'll always be my boys, no matter how old they get."

The rest of that day by the pool, and the next, was filled with non-stop talking, tall tales, and laughter. Generally, one player told stories about another player, but Bowden wasn't immune in any way.

One particular story involved Bowden's driving ability and the time he drove the team bus. It was Bowden's first year at South Georgia (1955), and all those who remembered his driving agreed that he was a much better coach than bus driver, especially on the curvy two-lane roads of northern Georgia. It seemed that Bowden frequently tried to take most of the curves without slowing down, and several times they nearly ended up in a ditch.

With tall tales being the order of the day, someone chimed in, "Yeah, it got so bad on one trip that we had to keep running from one side of the bus to the other just to keep it balanced so it wouldn't roll over."

Someone told stories about Bowden's short career as South Georgia's basketball coach and how he ended up firing himself when his team lost all their games but one.

Not even his wife and children were immune to a little joshing.

One story in particular that involved Ann and their youngest son, Terry, who was born in Douglas, centered on Terry's eating habits. According to the storyteller, while Bowden and his family were living in a small apartment on the first floor of Powell Hall (the dormitory where most of the football players lived), Ann would let their four kids play outside in the grassy area behind the building. Terry was the youngest, and he apparently had a sweet tooth. Knowing Terry's weakness, several of the players living in Powell Hall would buy candy or cookies at the student center, which was located next to the dormitory, and give it to him.

Terry was a little heavier than his siblings were when they were his age, and Ann was worried that all the sweets were the problem. Because she knew Terry ate more sweets when she wasn't outside with him, she made a sign that read "Do not feed" and taped it to the back of Terry's shirt before she let him go play. When she went to check on him, she noticed that his mouth was full and his pockets were stuffed. She discovered then that the sign she had made had been turned over and the message "Well Fed" written on it before it was re-taped to his shirt.

They told stories about their games too, especially the ones they used Bowden's trick plays in. And there were plenty of trick plays: fake pass plays (one was called the Statue of Liberty), fake punt plays, double reverses, and the lonely-end play. They even talked about one play they practiced repeatedly in 1956 but never used in a game. It was a defensive play that Bowden prepared in order to block field goals or extra points if it was necessary to win a game. In this play, Bull Smith literally threw Verlyn Giles over the line of scrimmage and into the line of flight of the kicked football. Verlyn Giles had been a tumbler in high school, and Bowden wasn't about to let any assets go unused.

Bowden didn't tell many stories himself, but he seemed to enjoy listening to them. He laughed as much as anyone, even when the stories were about him. The success of the weekend made it clear just how much these men cared about each other and enjoyed each other's fellowship. In fact, because it was such a success, they voted unanimously to reconvene at the same time and place in 1989.

Before their next reunion, the college offered to help plan a more structured schedule with a social hour at the president's residence, a golf match with Bowden, a tour of the college, a banquet at the college banquet hall, and, for the wives, a shopping trip with Ann Bowden (which has since become the source of several humorous stories itself). All of this has helped the "Bobby Bowden Reunion at South Georgia College" grow and become a big event that now includes anyone who ever played for him in any sport at South Georgia.

Although it was a biannual event in the beginning, in 1999 Bowden suggested that it should be every year, since none of them were getting any younger. It seemed that he realized without having to be reminded again that his boys were getting a little older. After he made the suggestion, there was an overwhelming vote to make it a yearly reunion, which it still is today.

It's no longer just a small group of former football players getting together with their coach to reminisce about old times. Now it includes the majority of the staff at South Georgia College, several local officials with an interest in the college, and every athlete who ever played for Bowden at South Georgia. It also frequently includes the kids and grandkids of many of those attending.

In many ways, it's become a big family affair as much as anything else. In fact, it has grown so big that Bowden spends a large portion of his time just signing autographs and posing for pictures. Even still, he remains the Tigers' old ball coach, and he spends as much time with his former players as he can.

Because of his personality, he's friendly to everyone, whether they're part of the reunion group or not, and this in itself consumes a lot of his time, especially since the people of Douglas still consider him to be one of their own, and they all feel comfortable approaching him when they see him.

Bowden's loving spirit has never changed and neither has his respect for his fellow man; it's an attitude and characteristic he's had all his life.

It's been said many times that the game of football builds character in young men. This is an oversimplification of what really happens. The real truth is that coaches like Bobby Bowden, who set positive examples in everything they do, both on and off the field, are responsible for building integrity and character in them. And all those men who Bowden still calls his "boys from South Georgia" know that this has always been his highest priority and his greatest goal.

He may not have known exactly how he was going to accomplish his goals when he started his career at South Georgia in 1955. His game plan may not have been as defined as he would have liked. But he knew that he was on a mission to serve God, so he made himself available, and as he has often said, "God has taken care of the rest."

A wise old minister once told his congregation that doing God's work is a lot like being in the watermelon business. A man in the watermelon business can easily count the number of seeds in one watermelon, and he usually knows how many seeds he needs every year to get a patch of watermelons. But he never knows for sure how many watermelons every seed will eventually produce, once it's germinated and reproducing.

This example can be used to illustrate the nature of Coach Bobby Bowden's life. He has been using his position as a football coach for over fifty years to influence young men in a positive way. And in doing that, he has been sowing seeds, and these seeds have been germinating and reproducing. As a result, he has touched the lives of an unbelievable number of young men and made them and their lives better.

Nobody knows the exact number except God, but a conservative estimate would be in the thousands, and it's safe to assume that this world is a better place because of his efforts.

After Coach Bowden retires and is called to Heaven, I'm sure that the Lord will say, "Welcome home, my good and faithful servant, you have done a good job."

It is also conceivable that when this happens, many of his boys from South Georgia College will be there to greet him.

ACKNOWLEDGEMENTS

This book would never have been written if it had not been for the encouragement and help of several wonderful people who, to this day, have amazed me with their keen recollection of what occurred more than one half century ago at a small college in southern Georgia. The humorous events that are depicted throughout these pages are those events that they were personally involved in or were aware of while they were attending South Georgia College. Because of their willingness to reveal some very personal aspects of their young lives, I am forever grateful and will always appreciate their candor.

In addition to interviewing these former students, whom I talked to time and time again, I also interviewed a large number of other former students and staff members, as well as several current staff members at South Georgia, all of whom graciously assisted me in researching the history of this school. Some of these individuals were James A. Cottingham, who is currently South Georgia's vice president for student affairs, and Ms. Pat Burch, who is currently employed as a librarian assistant. Both of these individuals made themselves available to assist me whenever I needed and requested it. I also interviewed Mr. Fred A. Birchmore, who was the dean of students in 1940 and 1941; Mr. Joe Davis, who was the head football coach in 1954; and three former students and football players: Colonel Joe W. Finley, U.S. Army Retired, who played football at South Georgia in 1941; Mr. Nathan H. Acker, who played in 1940 and 1941; and Mr. George A. Gaines, who played in 1938 and 1939.

To all of you, I appreciate your assistance. You made my experience researching the history of my alma mater more interesting and complete than I ever dreamed possible.

During my research, I also reviewed a multitude of official school records such as school annuals and quarterly bulletins, as well as hundreds of local newspaper articles written as far back as the 1920s, and, in particular, those written from 1954 through 1958. Most of those newspapers were being preserved on microfiche and were the official records of *The Douglas Enterprise* and *The Coffee County Progress*. Together they covered all of South Georgia's football games and any reportable event relating to their teams and football seasons. When I could locate them, I also reviewed and relied on *The South Georgian*, South Georgia's student newspaper, to refresh my frail and fading memory of those bygone years. All of these documents and newspapers were made available to me through the student library at South Georgia College, and again, I acknowledge gratefully that without the assistance of the entire library staff, I would never have been able to obtain the information needed to complete this book.

I am also indebted to those authors who wrote books previously published about Coach Bowden. Those books: *Bound For Glory* by Mike Bynum, *More Than Just A Game* by Bill Smith and Bobby Bowden, *Winning's Only Part Of The Game* by Ben Brown and the Bowden Family, and *The Bowden Way* by Steve Bowden and Bobby Bowden were always a valuable source of information and enlightenment as I tried to chronicle Coach Bowden's rise from a young boy in Birmingham, Alabama, to the legendary coach that he is today.

Of course none of this would have been possible without the permission and assistance of Coach Bowden. Thanks again, Coach, for everything you have done for me and all of my former teammates at South Georgia. None of us have ever been able to truly express in words what you and your beautiful wife, Ann, have meant to us for more than fifty years. Your enduring examples of a wonderful family, and the continuing love and respect that both of you constantly demonstrate have always been a beacon for us to follow.

I also want to thank Mary Ellen Bianco for her support and guidance in making this manuscript readable and grammatically correct.

And on a very personal note, I would be remiss if I failed to thank my wonderful wife, Dell, for allowing me the time away from her and my family to undertake this project, and for her tireless assistance in reading and rereading my manuscript as I pursued my goal of telling a story about my memories of a legend and his boys from South Georgia College.

ABOUT THE AUTHOR

It was in 1956 at South Georgia Junior College that Jimmy Bowen discovered the two great passions of his life: football and writing. Jimmy Bowen The Athlete played under the supervision of legendary head coach Bobby Bowden, learning lifelong lessons and forming friendships with truly extraordinary young men. Jimmy Bowen The Writer found his start in the printing room of the school's newspaper, where he worked as a member of the staff and a sports reporter. Despite his talent and proficiency in teaming these two subjects, he would not publish his first book for nearly fifty years.

Upon graduating in June of 1957, Bowen served on active duty with the U.S. Air Force for more than twelve years, working mainly as an investigator for the Office of Special Investigations. Even while committed to his duty, Bowen still made time to write, composing short stories for several base newspapers. Over the next couple decades, Bowen worked for the U.S. Treasury Department as a criminal investigator, and for the Federal Law Enforcement Training Center as a training instructor, where he wrote and contributed to several training manuals.

Since his graduation from South Georgia College, he has maintained a close, personal relationship with Coach Bowden and many of his former teammates. It was the privilege of belonging to this team that inspired him to write *Bobby Bowden: Memories of a Legend and His Boys from South Georgia College*, a challenge well worth the seven years Bowen spent completing it.

Jimmy Bowen currently lives in Louisville, Kentucky with his wife, Dell.